January 1994

So this Mark can
puum .... but can he
tube like our nephew
Sean — the expert tubster!

Happy Birthday Sean — we
hope you enjoy reading about someone
who likes the water as much as you!

Many happy returns from
Aunt Susan & Uncle Bob (Bullet)

Visions of Excellence

THE ART OF
ACHIEVING YOUR DREAMS

MARK TEWKSBURY

VIKING

VIKING
Published by the Penguin Group
Penguin Books Canada Ltd, 10 Alcorn Avenue, Toronto,
Ontario, Canada M4V 3B2
Penguin Books Ltd, 27 Wrights Lane, London W8 5TZ,
England
Viking Penguin, a division of Penguin Books USA Inc., 375
Hudson Street, New York, New York 10014, U.S.A.
Penguin Books Australia Ltd, Ringwood, Victoria, Australia
Penguin Books (NZ) Ltd, 182-190 Wairau Road, Auckland
10, New Zealand

Penguin Books Ltd, Registered Offices: Harmondsworth,
Middlesex, England

First published 1993

10 9 8 7 6 5 4 3 2 1
Copyright © Mark Tewksbury, 1993

Printed and bound in Canada on acid free paper ∞

Canadian Cataloguing in Publication Data
Tewksbury, Mark, 1968–
Visions of excellence: the art of achieving your dreams

ISBN 0-670-85192-2

1. Tewksbury, Mark, 1968–   . 2. Swimming.
3. Swimming – Biography.   I. Title.

GV838.T48A3 1993   797.2'1'092   C93-094023-7

ACKNOWLEDGEMENTS

Thanks first to my friends Carina Van Olm and Debbie without whose support and guidance I would have gone mad long ago. Your unconditional love has been the source of my strength.

To the gang at IMG, in particular Kevin Albrecht, Blake Corosky and Heather Jones, without whom I would never have been here in the first place.

To Cynthia Good, my publisher at Penguin, for believing I could write this book. And last but not least, to David Kilgour, my editor. I had no appreciation for the kind of work that goes into a book until we worked together.

INTRODUCTION

S ix one-hundredths of a second. That infini-
tesimal slice of time is how much faster than
Jeff Rouse I swam on July 30, 1992, and it
changed my life forever. It won me an Olympic
Gold Medal, put my face on the cover of *Time*,
brought me fame, launched me on a new career
and made me a role model for children across
Canada. It is why thousands of people come to
hear me speak, why they ask for my autograph,
why they want to hear my story and why you
picked up this book.

The external measure of excellence in sport is
pretty simple. Whoever swims the fastest,
throws the farthest or jumps the highest is the
best. I am proud of those six one-hundredths of
a second. But there is also an internal kind of
excellence that is far more difficult to measure.
It comes with all the blood, sweat and tears that
lead to winning. After all, I worked sixteen years
for that fraction of a second.

In the year since my victory in Barcelona, I have made motivational speeches to more than one hundred thousand people. Everywhere I go people ask me how I did it. They also want to know about me. This book is intended to answer both questions. It is partly about my life as a swimmer, partly about the principles I applied to achieve excellence. I suppose it could be called a motivational memoir.

Seventeen years ago I was a perfectly ordinary kid. I still think of myself as ordinary. But I had a vision of excellence and I was lucky enough to achieve it. What has amazed me about the response to my achievement is the overwhelming outpouring of emotion from complete strangers who have taken me to their hearts. When I describe my experiences in speeches, the audiences laugh and cry with me every step of the way. Wherever I go in Canada, people come up to me in the street and call me Mark as if we were friends. Time and again I've asked myself why my accomplishment moves people so deeply and personally. I believe the fact that I achieved my dream gives them hope that they will realize their own dreams.

We all have our own visions of excellence; mine grew out of my experience as a swimmer, and so the stories you'll read in this book are about swimming. But I believe the principles they illuminate can be applied by anyone pursuing a dream, whether it's starting up a business, succeeding in school, or even getting through a job interview. I have learned enormously this last year from the people who have shared their dreams with me, and I hope this book gives something back. It is through sharing that we all become more enriched. I know. I saw a skinny, unco-ordinated kid transformed because his imagination was awakened by the excellence of others.

Mark Tewksbury
Calgary
July 1993

Visions of Excellence

Nothing But a Dreamer

"From a little spark might burst
a big flame."
DANTE

W HEN I WAS A CHILD I LIVED IN A WORLD where anything seemed possible. I dreamed the impossible and believed that one day it would come true. Like most kids I took things for granted. I didn't appreciate how protected and limited my life was.

With time my perspective has changed. Needless to say, I am not so innocent any more, certainly not as naïve, but I still try to retain that optimistic outlook I had when I was six years old. It was important for me because it set the course my life would take for the next sixteen years. Recently I have been reminded of that open attitude to life by spending time with children.

A friend of mine has kids aged three and seven, and I enjoy having them visit because I learn from watching them. Andrew, the three-year-old, picks up anything remotely interesting and turns it into something he can play with. My Dustbuster becomes a spaceship, a shoe becomes a car, and my paper-clips become a long, winding silver snake. Cayley watches as her brother bolts around the room but bombards me with questions instead of joining him. She asks, "What's this?" about everything. She listens to my answers then replies with her own ideas. If I show her a picture of a horse she says, "I'm going to ride a horse this summer." If I show her some memorabilia from the Olympics, she responds, "I'm going to be in the Olympics one day." She is full of hope and ambition. And as I watch them play, I realize both she and her brother have the ability to dream.

It seems that all kids have that ability. When I was in grade school I saw my first picture of an astronaut during one of my science classes. The rest of the day I was in space, literally. I couldn't help myself, the video had me hooked. I dreamed of becoming an astronaut.

This lasted a good two months, until members of the local fire department visited our school. They wore impressive fire-proof suits and huge helmets; they got to slide down poles and ride in fire engines. The space program had been intriguing, but here was a fireman, in the flesh. I was convinced. A fireman I would be.

Looking back on that time, I now realize how important school and role models were in helping develop my dreams. I was so young and unsuspecting, I didn't know any better than to think whatever I wanted would come true. I was a boundless dreamer who saw no obstacles, why I don't know. Kids seem to have this universal trait of imagining the impossible, no matter how ordinary their surroundings.

My childhood was unremarkable, as was I. I was the oldest in a family of three children, and we moved every year until I was nine, so I lived in a series of two-bedroom bungalows in different suburban areas. In school I was always the new kid, which made me feel insecure. I wasn't very athletic; in fact, I wasn't good at most sports. I dreaded playing team sports like soccer because I was inevitably the last one picked. Why I continued to dream, and dream so vividly, may seem a puzzle, but I think it may have been the very smallness and ordinariness of my life that made the dream so important, so real to me.

I now wonder when it is that many of us lose that wonderful sense of imagination. When do we lose the ability to dream? Maybe it isn't so much the *when* as the *why*. Do we give up dreaming because it's too disappointing, because it hurts too much if we don't achieve it? Is it because we don't have the skills needed to make the dreams come true or are we just so satisfied with the status quo we don't feel the need to push for anything more?

Some people never seem to stop dreaming. They are the extraordinary ones you see in the news passing milestones. Roberta Bondar travels in space, Rick Hanson takes his "Man in

Motion" tour around the world, Wayne Gretzky continues to dominate the National Hockey League. They continually make the headlines because they keep reaching for new heights and surpassing them.

When I was growing up, television played a big role in moulding my dreams. I wasn't allowed to watch too much TV, but I saw enough to realize that anything was possible. It brought the Gretzkys of the world into my living room and exposed me to their achievements. When I saw what was possible for others, it made me dream of doing it myself.

In the summer of 1976, when I was eight years old, a monumental event changed my life. The Olympic Games were held in Montreal, and on July 17th my family, along with millions of other Canadians, watched the opening cere-monies on TV. We then spent the next two weeks riveted to the television set. I really had no idea what the Olympics were about, I just knew they were a sports event, but as we sat and watched the ceremonies I became mesmer-ized. What really impressed me was the number of countries represented and the athletes marching. It seemed as though the parade would never end. I kept wondering when we would see the athletes from our own country.

Finally, the last nation marched into the stadium. It was Canada. The crowd erupted and it was like nothing I had ever seen before. Abby Hoffman led the team, carrying the flag. It was an incredibly moving sight. My family was very quiet, silently soaking in every emotion we saw displayed on the screen. People in the crowd were smiling and waving, a few were even crying. I sat spellbound.

For the next sixteen days I was allowed to watch as much television as I wanted, and I became completely committed to the games. During the first seven days I watched the swimming. The Canadians didn't win gold but they were very close, time after time. I remember watching Nancy Garapick win the first of her two bronzes in the backstroke, Cheryl Gibson win a silver medal in the 400 individual medley and Graham Smith win a bronze with his teammates on the relay.

It was the medal ceremonies that really moved me. They were such a celebration, full of pageantry and splendour. The swimming medallists would march from one end of the pool down towards the podium. Somebody important would be introduced as the presenter. The Queen was often at the pool and took part in the celebrations. I remember the faces of the athletes waiting to receive their medals. There was such anticipation, then joy, smiles and even tears. The crowd would stand for the playing of the winner's national anthem and the three flags of the medallist countries would be raised. I never heard the Canadian anthem but I saw many Canadian flags being raised. It left a lasting impression.

The second week of the games was filled with track and field. I watched as Diane Jones competed in five different events. I watched as Greg Joy had a magnificent high jump. I loved his last name because I associated it with the games. I remember hearing about something called a boycott but not really understanding what it meant. My parents explained that some countries, African countries, had chosen not to compete in the games. I also remember the gymnastic competition and like the rest of the world, I couldn't keep my eyes off a girl called Nadia.

On August 1st, the 19th Olympiad came to a close, and I was sorry to see the end of it. Something in me had been awakened; never had I been so inspired by anything. Every night I would go to bed and dream about the games because finally I had seen something that I thought I might actually be able to do. Although I wasn't good at sports, I did at least know how to swim.

Three years earlier, when I was five years old, my father, an accountant for an oil company, had been transferred to Dallas, Texas, and we lived there for a year and a half. I don't remember a lot, but a few things stand out. I remember going to my first drive-in. I recall bugs the size of my little brother, Scott. But the most memorable thing was the heat. It was so hot down there we did anything we could to cool off. Fortunately our townhouse complex had an outdoor swimming pool, and my mother would take all three of us kids—Scott, two years old, Colleen, three, and me—down to the pool every day. I learned to swim there.

When we came back to Canada I asked my parents to enrol me in a swim club, but the timing wasn't right. I loved swimming but I was too young to be in an official, supervised program. Every time I went to the pool I wanted my family there to watch me. This was hard on my mother because she had to look after my brother and sister, and impossible for my father because he had to work. After a couple of weeks my parents decided to wait until I was older to let me join any sort of club.

After seeing the Olympics on television, a year later, and given that I had already swum and knew I liked it, I found a new dream. I no longer wanted to be an astronaut or a fireman. I wanted to be a swimmer in the Olympic Games. When I returned to school in September I told everybody that I would be in the Olympics one day. My teacher looked at me a little sadly. I'm sure she had heard this a hundred times on the first day of classes, but I don't think any other kid had meant it as much as I did. Later in September I went to practise at the Cascade Swim Club and I didn't ask my family to watch. This time I had all the inspiration I needed.

For me, this is when it all started. I couldn't stop myself from thinking about the Olympics. I was only eight years old, but I had the ability to dream.

I sometimes wonder what separated me from all the other kids I started swimming with. Why did I end up at the Olympics? I wasn't from a family of natural athletes. My parents never pushed me to become a champion, and we weren't rich enough to buy the best training money could buy. We were just an average family. There was nothing extraordinary about me, except that I had found something that inspired me. It was the dream that ultimately set me apart.

Of course, not all dreams lead to success or fulfilment. I have had too many dreams to count. As a young child I dreamed of doing countless things other than swimming. My first dream was to fit in, to be good at something, anything, so people would like me. I wanted to be able to play hockey or soccer or to be smarter. I wanted to play the saxophone or be an actor, but I was tone deaf, and my school had no acting classes. My dreams in those areas were squashed, but I kept trying to find a new dream, which I think is a normal human reaction to disappointment. I knew instinctively that without a dream I would have no chance of succeeding, and that kept me coming back to the idea of the Olympics. I was naturally good at swimming—not great, but good—and that made me feel I fit in. When all my other dreams faded, my vision of swimming at the Olympics stayed with me. Over the years it remained one of the few constants in my life.

Some people never lose that child's ability to dream; they are the lucky ones, even if at times they fail. The real failure comes only if they never dream again.

SUMMARY

Dreaming

Anything is possible with dreams.
Don't be afraid to dream the impossible.

"May the dreams of your past
be the reality of your future."
ANONYMOUS

2

Seeing Is Believing

"What you see is what you get."
ANONYMOUS

M Y OLYMPIC DREAM WAS A CRUCIAL PART OF my vision, but it was only the first component. It quickly became clear to me that there was a lot more necessary to complete the picture. My first experience at the swim club was a shock. I had thought I would represent Canada in the next Olympics, four years from 1976. It never occurred to me that I would only be able to swim a couple of lengths when I started. During the early stages I was absorbed with just trying to survive in the pool! Every workout I learned something new, and the more I learned, the better I understood that my dream was going to take a very long time to achieve.

At first I clearly held onto my memories of the 1976 Olympics, but it didn't take long for them to fade. The reality of my situation made my long-term goal seem completely out of focus. Instead of always thinking about the Olympics I had to look at short-term goals. It had never occurred to me that before I could be the best swimmer in the world I would have to be the best in my club, then the best in the city and so on. More importantly, before I could be the best in the club I would have to *see* myself as being the best.

Two months after joining the club I started competing against the other twenty boys and girls in the beginners' group. The coach would set up short one- or two-length races in all four strokes: the butterfly, backstroke, breaststroke and freestyle. I found this intimidating because I could only swim one stroke well—the freestyle. Standing on the pool deck, waiting for the start of my race, I would be terrified, afraid of failing in front of my new friends. I lacked a certain level of self-confidence that was necessary to be competitive. To me this felt like being picked for soccer all over again.

In some of the races, the breaststroke in particular, I was always last. I could never swim this stroke. But in other events, like the freestyle, I usually placed in the top three. Because we were all beginners, none of us was good at everything. Over all we seemed to be pretty evenly matched. I didn't give up, because although I was hopeless in some events, I knew I was competitive in others.

As I became a better swimmer, over the following two years, my self-confidence improved, and by the time I was ten I approached racing differently. Instead of being petrified with fear, I could see myself succeeding. My confidence enabled me to see a positive outcome before I even started the swim. I learned that before I competed I needed to do two types of warm-up—a physical one for the body and a visual one for the mind.

Intuitively I began seeing each race before I swam it. I tried to imagine positive results in my mind so that when I went in to race I would be in control. Without knowing it, I was using what is now known as visualization. This skill provided me with the opportunity to see excellence before I actually achieved it.

INCORPORATING VISUALIZATION INTO COMPETITION

To be an effective visualizer required a lot of concentration. Before a race I would escape the crowds and noise for a while, sitting quietly, focusing on what I was about to do. I tried to picture the upcoming race in my mind, taking myself through it one step at a time. I would close my eyes and see myself on the starting block. The starter would give me the command, "Take your marks," and I would hear a gun going off. I tried to picture myself having a perfect dive into the pool. I would come up out of the water strongly and start swimming with perfect technique. I would picture the turn, then the last part of the race, and I could see myself finishing strongly in my mind's eye. My goal was to close my eyes and try to finish the race mentally in the same time it would actually take to physically swim the race. It didn't always work, but this was the goal. When I finished and I opened my eyes, I would feel a bit sluggish, as if I'd been wakened from a deep sleep. This feeling passed and by the time I went to race, I would be so focused my body could go on autopilot. It would follow the plan I had seen in my mind.

When I first started doing this, it was frustrating and exhausting. I would close my eyes and try to picture the race and nothing would come. Sometimes I fell asleep instead of visualizing! Other times I would try to picture myself swimming and all I could see were my competitors. Even worse, sometimes, when I had successfully pictured myself doing well, I would get in the race and panic when the first little thing didn't go according to my plan.

With time I learned to become more sophisticated in my visualizing skills. It was very important to picture myself clearly through each step of the race, but it was also important to include external factors. For example, it would be ideal if I was the only competitor, but this just wasn't the case. To visualize effectively I had to have some idea in my mind that there would be other people in the race. I didn't focus on them too much, but I needed to be aware of them so that they wouldn't distract mc during the swim. I even learned to go through my race plan and imagine something bad happening. Then I would immediately respond to the situation in my mind, so that if it happened during the race, I would be able to react effectively.

Of course, I always tried to picture myself winning. In order to do this I had to imagine the others behind me. Sometimes the thought of winning was very frightening. It took a long time to train my mind to see myself being the best. At every level of competition this was the hardest thing to overcome. Once I could imagine myself being the best in my city, I had to make the transition to see myself being the best in the province, until finally I had to see myself being the best in the world. I was competing internationally for many years before this became possible.

The ability to visualize doesn't happen overnight. It can take years to perfect, but by persevering you can eventually see the desired outcome clearly and absolutely in your mind, whether it's imagining yourself giving a speech to a room full of strangers, answering difficult questions in a job interview, or standing on the top podium in a victory ceremony.

WHEN DREAMS COME TO LIFE—
AND WHEN THEY FAIL

Using visualization before a competition became second nature to me. My preparation time took more than an hour for a race that was completed in less than a minute. I would visualize my race continually during this time. Even with these skills success did not come overnight. It took a couple of years to be the best in my swim club, and three before I was the best swimmer in my city, then another two until I was the best in the province. After swimming for eight years, I finally reached the stage where I could start to focus on being the best in Canada.

Each progression was important. My strength didn't lie only in my technical swimming skills; it was in the ability to combine them with the power of my mind. By the time I became the best swimmer in the province my confidence and training had risen to a level where I could see myself taking the next step, trying to be the best in the country. At the same time, a transition was possible only because I was *physically and mentally* ready. It was never one without the other.

When I finally became the best in Canada I found the last advancement, to be the best in the world, very difficult. This was an entirely "foreign" thought to me. I could imagine myself being the best within the borders of my own country, but I had a hard time seeing myself as the best in the *world*. It was too immense a field.

This became obvious in 1988. Swimming in Montreal at the very pool I had seen on television in 1976, one of my childhood dreams came true. I qualified to represent Canada in the 24th Summer Olympics to be held at the end of September in Seoul, Korea. Our team would assemble for training camps sporadically and would eventually come together as a unit at the end of August.

On September 10th, the Canadian swim team flew to Seoul. Korean women in traditional dress greeted us as we got off the plane, and we were taken to the Olympic village on a big bus painted with Olympic symbols. There was a police escort leading the way so we could rush through traffic. People in cars waved as we drove through streets lined with flags decorated with Olympic rings and emblems. It was just as I imagined it would be.

I spent the first two days exploring the Olympic village and was struck by how gigantic it was. The cafeteria was three storeys high and could seat four thousand people. The indoor pool could seat more than eight thousand people and must have taken up the size of six city blocks. There were movie theatres, arcades and even a shopping centre. I was impressed by all the amenities the village offered. It was like living in our own city within Seoul.

Unfortunately, the novelty wore off quickly and over the next five days I became disillusioned with the village. The food was monotonous, exactly the same meals served every single day. After a week, I could barely stomach the food. With new national teams arriving daily, the village was filling up and becoming exceptionally noisy. There were approximately twelve thousand people living in close quarters and the village was alive day and night. Trying to get to sleep became an ordeal. As more people arrived, the line-ups for food became longer and longer and it was frustrating to have to wait upwards of thirty minutes in queues. (And I had thought there would be room service!)

Living in the village was distracting, and as each day passed, I became less confident. I felt in awe of most of the people around me and became unfocused. I was so intimidated I found it hard to meet other athletes. As a rookie I should have shared some of my feelings with my team-mates, but as my nervousness grew I became more introverted. Besides, most of my room-mates were rookies, too, and I couldn't really turn to them because they were as awestruck as I was. I feared that my nervousness might be perceived as weakness so I remained silent.

The games were to officially open on September 17th. The night before the ceremonies, I looked out of my window in the village and noticed the Chinese team lined up in perfect rows of ten, practising marching for the next day. I felt kind of sorry for them, having to endure such a strict regimen, but the next day, as our time came to march around the stadium, I appreciated what the Chinese had been up to the night before. We were instructed to line up in neat rows of ten. Carolyn Waldo, the gold medal favourite in synchronized swimming, was at the front, carrying the flag and leading the way. The representatives of the Canadian Olympic Association were next, followed by the women's team and then the men's.

We tried to form lines of ten but no one wanted to be in the middle. The television cameras focused on the people on the outside, so everyone was vying for these positions. We were in groups of two or three instead of lines of ten. Carolyn started waving the flag back and forth, then began to march. I remember hearing them announce Canada and thinking to myself, "We aren't ready yet," but suddenly we were in the stadium. Events weren't unfolding as perfectly as I had pictured they would.

My main event, the 100-metre backstroke, was to take place on September 24th. The swimming began on September 18th, so for six days I sat and watched others compete. After the races I would swim my workout of the day. This was the most crowded time because most athletes followed the same schedule. It only made me more anxious because I was training with most of my competitors, and I saw how impressively they were performing. Every day I would leave the pool feeling exhausted. I was wasting my energy becoming engrossed in others' races and focusing on my competitors. As my swim loomed closer, my confidence was at a low ebb.

As a country, we were having a frustrating time in the pool. Canadians made it to a lot of finals but weren't making it to the medal podium. The great Victor Davis, a gold medal favourite in the breaststroke, came fourth in a close race. Alison Higson, another medal hope in the same event, swam a personal best but also finished fourth. It seemed that no matter how hard we tried, or how well we swam, we were destined to be fourth or fifth. I was becoming disheartened. If none of my team-mates were winning medals, how on earth could I?

The night before my swim, I went to bed but sleep never came. I was thinking about the race too much. In the morning I went to eat early, to avoid the crowds, and walked over to the pool. I did my physical warm-up and then got ready mentally for my first race of the day.

What happens at the Olympics is this: there are fifty to sixty athletes from around the world who qualify for any given event. In the morning we swim in heats. These are like elimination rounds, except you only get one shot. The top eight performers in the morning's heats compete in the evening final for the medals.

At the end of the heats I was tied for sixth place. Although relieved to have qualified for the final, I was frustrated because I knew that I had given everything I had in the morning. It would take a miracle for me to win a medal.

I went back to my room in the village and tried to sleep during the eight-hour break between the heats and the final. I was very tired from not sleeping the night before, but I was thinking too much, and once again, I could not sleep. For hours I lay there trying to visualize myself winning but the image just wouldn't come.

That evening, before the race, the finalists gathered in the "ready room." It is a small area, about ten feet by twelve feet, with eight chairs and four concrete walls, where the finalists spend the last thirty minutes before their race. Needless to say, the feeling in this room is extremely tense. You can be the fittest athlete in the world, but if you can't concentrate under these stressful circumstances you don't stand a chance.

All eight people are after the same thing; they all want to win. Usually before a race I put a towel over my head and go through my visualization process. In Seoul I didn't do this. For thirty minutes I sat there and was completely distracted by my competitors. I watched as two Russian swimmers pointed at me and said "Nyet, nyet." I was in awe of Daichi Suzuki, the Japanese swimmer, who was doing deep knee squats and jumping almost to the roof. I felt the way I had years earlier standing on the pool deck as an eight-year-old: petrified. I didn't want to fail, but as hard as I tried, I couldn't focus on the upcoming race.

After a half-hour the chief marshal came in and lined us up. As always, the Olympic music was played as we walked through the doors that led to the starting end of the pool. In the distance I could hear the roar of the crowd. Because I was in lane one, I was the first finalist to be introduced. When I heard my name I waved to the stands, then I stopped listening to the announcers and tried to get ready to race.

Those last few minutes were odd. Usually I would be so focused on visualizing myself succeeding that I wouldn't notice anything around me. On this night I couldn't stop being distracted and couldn't see any picture in my mind. Strangely, I felt no excitement whatsoever. For the past week I had watched from the stands as the finalists were being marched out, anticipating the time when it would be my turn. I had felt nervous just thinking about it. Now I was standing here, this was my final, and I didn't feel anything.

I don't remember much about the race. Towards the end I could hear a roar from the crowd in the distance. I was ahead of the swimmer in lane two, but I knew the cheering wasn't for me. When I hit the wall at the end of the race I looked immediately to the scoreboard to see the results. Usually, I look for my name but this time I looked to see who had won. Obviously it wasn't me. That honour went to the Japanese swimmer, Daichi Suzuki, king of the deep knee squats. He had miraculously beaten the

American David Berkoff, who had set a world record that morning. I had come fifth.

After the race I still didn't feel much. It was as though the entire swim had happened without me. I was physically there but mentally absent.

The next day, I swam in the medley relay with three of my team-mates. Thanks to the efforts of those three, Victor Davis, Tom Ponting and Sandy Goss, I won an Olympic medal. We came second, and I took part in a medal ceremony after all. I really didn't have a lot to do with winning, though. The other guys had the swims of their lives to put me on the podium.

I left Seoul with mixed emotions. In one sense, these games had fulfilled the dream I'd held for so long—I had won a medal. On the other hand, in my individual performance I had completely given up on myself. I had dreamed of going to the Olympics and being my best. When I finally got there it hadn't happened.

STARTING BACK SLOWLY

Coming back to Canada in the fall of 1988 I felt torn. Should I continue swimming or should I quit? I took time off both swimming and school but ended up feeling even more lost. I didn't have any goals, nothing to focus on. I could no longer picture the games as I had as a child; the romanticized version was gone. When I thought about the Olympics now I felt very disillusioned.

I almost retired from swimming during this period. I was twenty years old, and ready to resume my studies full time at the University of Calgary. I had put my life on hold and now wanted to start living again. My self-confidence was low and I didn't think I had the strength to survive the stress of training. I had no clear vision in my mind. Without a dream and a focus I didn't see any point in continuing.

One thing kept me from quitting. If being fifth in the Olympics was the best I could do, I could have stopped competing with ease. What I couldn't live with was the fact that I had given up on myself: after years of visualizing success I had had no image on the most important day of all. I decided I had to keep competing, at least for a while, until I regained my self-confidence. Otherwise I knew I would regret it for the rest of my life.

In the winter of 1989 I started swimming again. I went back to the basics I had practised many years earlier. Whenever I entered a competition I forced myself to visualize. My psyche was very fragile for the first while, and I found it hard to see myself winning anything. Although I didn't know it at the time, that would change. I had all the tools for success already in place, and I only needed the confidence to use them effectively.

I became braver in my visualization as I started to have some success. By the end of 1989 I could start to see myself winning again and I decided to give swimming another chance. I committed to another three years because I felt this time I would be able to see myself being the best in the world.

LEARNING TO VISUALIZE
THE RESULT YOU DESIRE

In 1992, as I was getting ready for the Barcelona Olympics, I again tried to visualize the race in my mind. This time it was easy to imagine the final. I had been there before, so I could picture it clearly.

As I closed my eyes I could see the ready room. I saw the other finalists as we were getting ready to march to the pool. I heard the Spanish crowd in the distance, I felt the heat of the sun on my face. There was one problem: every time I imagined the results on the scoreboard I saw myself placing fifth. After all, I was imagining everything so vividly because I'd been to the Olympics before and come fifth. Every time I pictured my swim in Barcelona this is what I imagined.

In March of 1992 I became worried that I wouldn't ever be able to picture myself coming first in Barcelona. I could not erase the image of Seoul from my mind. I decided the only way to see my desired result would be to travel to Barcelona to see the Olympic pool well beforehand. If I could do that, I hoped I'd wipe the slate clean and start to visualize a different outcome.

On March 2nd I travelled to Barcelona with Trevor Tiffany, a friend from Swimming/Natation Canada. Trevor was the technical director of SNC and he understood how important it was for me to make the trip.

We went directly from the airport to the Olympic pool complex. The facility, while not yet finished, was already impressive. The warm-up pool was indoors, the competition pool outdoors. This was different from the complex in Seoul, which was completely indoors, and it would make an enormous difference to me. Because I swim the backstroke, I use the roof of a pool to guide me but this is impossible outdoors. I tried to imagine where the sun would be in the evening for the final and made a mental note. The picture in my mind was becoming a little clearer.

I stood up in the stands looking at the pool for a long time. Eventually I went down and stood on the deck. I walked from where I thought the ready room would be out to lane four and I waved to the imaginary crowd. In fact there were only thirty Spanish construction workers in the stands but I saw thousands of people in my mind. I then walked back to the ready room and went through the same procedure to lane five. These were the only two lanes I was interested in because on July 30th they would be assigned to the top two qualifiers, lane four for the first, lane five for the second. I thought if I really were to have a shot at winning the race, I would have to be in one of these two lanes.

I stood there and I let my imagination run wild. I pictured winning in this pool. I imagined the feeling I would have when I looked up at the scoreboard and my name had the number one beside it. It was so exhilarating I had goosebumps just thinking about it.

When we left the pool I could finally lay the ghost of 1988 to rest. This pool was very different from the one in Seoul. When I next imagined this summer's swim I would remember what I had seen today. I would start to look at the future.

The rest of the day Trevor took me around the city to soak up the atmosphere. I made journal entries as we drove so I wouldn't forget what I was seeing. My journal entry for March 2nd reads: Travelled to Barcelona today. Went to the pool and it is perfect. I have a good sense of what the Olympics will be like now. This trip was very worthwhile. I not only have a clear image of the pool, I have also seen the city. I have a new vision. These are going to be my Olympics.

SUMMARY

Visualization

Imagine yourself succeeding.

Visualization helps improve self-confidence.

The mind is a powerful factor in everything you do.

"Man has his future within him, dynamically alive at this very moment."
ABRAHAM MASLOW

3

This Isn't a Dream, This Is a Nightmare

"If you have built castles in the air,
your work need not be lost;
that is where they should be.
Now put foundations under them."
HENRY DAVID THOREAU

V ISUALIZING MADE IT EASIER TO REMAIN focused but it didn't help me through some of the tough times when it seemed the easiest thing would be to give up, to stop struggling.

Very shortly after I started swimming, I was faced with some of the drudgery that was part of the daily routine. Being a swimmer included going to morning workouts. Getting up at five in the morning was never easy for me. When I was younger, before I could drive, I used to go to bed at night and pray my parents would sleep through their alarm so they wouldn't get up to take me to practice. I suffered many sleepless nights thinking about how tired I would be the next day. My ability to focus was a strength, but it could also be a weakness if I looked only at the negative.

Eventually I wasn't dependent on anybody to get me to the pool. Once the alarm went off I went to practice, even if I wanted to sleep in, and in many years of practising, I rarely missed. I learned to focus on the positive. I had made a commitment to my team and to myself and this was a part of that commitment.

As I got older, things didn't get any easier. In junior and senior high school, when most of my friends would hang out after classes, I would go straight to the pool. More than anything I wanted to be just one of the guys, but I always had practice after school as well as before.

In grade eight I was surrounded by a good group of people. Most of my friends were athletic and understood why I was busy after school. A lot of them played football and basketball for the school team and had their own practices to go to. On weekends we would get together and see movies, go to parties, or just spend time. I was never lacking for friends.

Halfway through the year I started going on weekend trips to competitions. I would come back to school on Monday and hear about the great times I missed when I was away. With each passing weekend I felt myself becoming more alienated from my peers. This really upset me but there wasn't anything I could do. No matter what I did, life for them went on while I was away. By the time spring came, my friends and I didn't have much in common and we stopped hanging out together.

This tended to be the pattern of my adolescence. In grade nine I went to a new school, and it was impossible to form close friendships because of my schedule. Sometimes the sacrifice seemed too great. My days consisted of swimming, school, eating and sleeping, and it seemed as though every day was carefully planned. I could never be irresponsible and just do something at the last minute. There was always that five A.M. wake-up call looming, or that practice after school to attend. This regimented lifestyle alienated me from my schoolmates. It wasn't easy being different and there were many times I felt like a loser. Yet for one reason or another, I was always drawn back to the pool.

However, going to the pool wasn't always easy, either. When I was in my early teens, I had a coach whose son was my age and was very competitive with me. It became obvious who was going to receive the better coaching. This man did everything he could to promote his own son instead of helping me improve. He was known to play favourites and was sometimes abusive.

I was determined not to let this coach ruin swimming for me. If anything, he made me that much more intent on making something of myself. I had to work twice as hard to get any recognition. I had to be twice as tough not to give up when he would criticize me in front of the rest of the club. This is not an unusual experience.

By the time an athlete gets to the top of his or her sport he or she is likely to have had at least half a dozen coaches. Inevitably, whether it be due to personality clashes or differences in training philosophy, or some other reason, there are going to be conflicts that have to be resolved. If they are irreconcilable, you have to take action. In my case, I put up with the situation for more than a year before I decided that I had had enough. My only option was to join the competition.

TAKING A RISK

Calgary had two major swim clubs when I was growing up. The competition, the University of Calgary Swim Club, was on the opposite side of the city from where I lived. I was fourteen years old when I joined and scared to death. As much as I hadn't liked my old club, I had been comfortable there. I knew what to expect. Going to this new club was a big risk for me but I really felt I had no choice.

I had heard rumours that this club worked swimmers so hard that you were lucky to last a week with them. They had an incredible range of talent, from young swimmers all the way up to a varsity swimming program. I had even heard that breaststroker Graham Smith, a legend and one of my idols from the 1976 Olympics, was swimming there. How would I ever survive among such stars?

When I arrived I found the work wasn't much different from my other program. Like my former

club, there were different groups that had vary-
ing workout schedules. There was a group that
swam incredible distances, but I wasn't placed
in it. Instead, I swam in the youth group with
thirty other athletes my age. Even though the
workouts were more rigorous and the travel
time to and from practices was greater, this club
had a totally different spirit and my pre-con-
ceived horrors were soon laid to rest. There was
a sense of excitement and, for the first time, I
was part of a peer group that accepted me for
who I was. I was silly, I made people laugh, I
came alive. I finally felt I belonged.

In this new atmosphere I flourished and within two years I was swimming with the top group.
During the Christmas holidays of 1984, when I
was sixteen, I was part of a training program
commonly referred to as "hell week," which actually consisted of ten ten-hour days. We started
with four hours of swimming and five hours of
"land work." The other hour was broken into two
fifteen-minute breaks and a half-hour for lunch.
As the days progressed we increased the swimming time and decreased the land program. On
the last day the plan was to swim a marathon,
forty kilometres, in ten hours.

This ten-day stretch was like nothing I had
ever been through before. It wasn't the swimming

that was so difficult. It was the land work combined with the swimming that made it so challenging. I was so sore from weights and floor hockey and running circuits that I could barely move in the pool. As each day went on, our fatigue deepened. Having no days off made it impossible to recover.

This training camp was designed to do two things. First, we were pushed harder physically than we ever had been before. At the end of the ten days we would be in the best shape of our lives. Second, our mental strength was being challenged. We were trained to the point of breaking daily and then we had to come back, fourteen hours later, and start all over again. Our coach, Deryk Snelling, wanted to make us so strong that even if things were extremely hard in an international competition, we wouldn't give up.

By the second-last day of this camp, the physical emphasis was laid solely on swimming. We weren't doing any land work but we were swimming thirty-five kilometres daily. We were so sore and tired nobody really talked after half the day was over. It made more sense to save our energy. I went home at night and literally fell asleep at the dinner table. I was totally exhausted.

With one day to go, our coach gave us a motivational talk. His mood was positive, but he reminded us that we still had a whole day left to complete the training. This would be the hardest yet. We were going to try to swim a marathon, more than forty kilometres, in one day. Starting at eight the next morning we would work towards the goal and would swim until it was completed, ten hours later.

I had never faced a challenge quite like this before, and I was anxious and excited when I arrived at the pool the next morning. But for some members of the team the accumulation of the previous work, coupled with the fear of this challenge, was too much, and they failed to show up.

The day was fierce. At one point I was so tired and discouraged I actually started crying while I was swimming. I didn't know what else to do; the pain was unbearable. We weren't just swimming back and forth, we were performing exceptionally challenging sets. We'd been told to eat raisins and drink juice all day to keep our energy high. I remember the turn-around time between sets was so short I shoved a handful of nuts and raisins into my mouth, but didn't have time to swallow. I just chewed and chewed and then pushed off the wall and started swimming.

The poor guy behind me swam through all this gross mixture in the water. To this day I cringe when I see raisins.

During the afternoon session we started to lose people. The sugar levels in their bodies dropped to the point where they couldn't function any more. One boy was particularly stricken. He was so disoriented that he didn't realize when he had come to the end of the pool. His head was up against the wall and he should have already completed a turn and started a new length, but instead of turning he just kept swimming. His arms were hitting the pool deck. Deryk had to pull his face up out of the water to tell him to stop swimming, and when he finally came out of his daze he had to get out.

As the number of swimmers slowly dwindled, it became more challenging to keep going. It was hard to stay motivated when I could see other people getting out. They weren't quitting, their bodies just didn't have any more energy. It made me want to give up too. There was a constant inner struggle. Half of me wanted to give up, while the other half didn't, but somehow the challenge of finishing kept me going.

At 6:15 that evening the workout ended. Twenty-three of the original thirty who had started accomplished our goal. In just over ten hours we had swum our marathon. I went home, got straight into bed, and slept for sixteen hours.

Many people wondered why we would ever do this to ourselves, and they thought our coach was sadistic. But for me, this day proved to be a great breakthrough. It taught me that if you persevere you can go great distances and surprise yourself. Two weeks earlier, if somebody had asked me if I could last through the training camp I would have immediately said no. Yet here I was, and I had made it. I realized that sometimes I put limits on myself by what I thought I could and couldn't accomplish.

MIND OVER MATTER

Through ever-greater challenges I learned some important things. Whatever your dream is, there is no way to avoid the work. That is the first step in taking action towards the goal. But I also saw that it is more than just the action. It is rising to the challenges that present themselves along the way that leads to victory. By working hard and persevering through both failure and success, my belief in myself was once again fuelled. After training, I felt I deserved to perform well in competition because my preparation had been successfully completed.

Later in 1985, after the Christmas training camp, I made my first big breakthrough in the international swimming circuit. I had emerged as a specialist in the backstroke and I swam a time in my event, the 100-metre, that catapulted me from forty-third to fourth in the world. I was seventeen years old.

Over the next seven years I would remain one of the world's better swimmers, but never its best. I tended to hover between third and fourth place, which was quite an achievement, but I never reached number one, which was always my goal. I became content with fourth position. It felt safe. It was comfortable to be good but not the best. Ranked fourth I always had a shot at winning a medal in an international event, but I was never expected to place first. There is a big difference between the two.

The journey from second to first required a completely different mindset. Even though I was only a few positions and merely tenths of seconds away from being the best, I was in a different league. The act of will needed to believe you are the best in the entire world is enormous. It was always easier for me to be slightly behind the leaders.

Because I had experienced how hard it was to get to fourth position I knew how difficult it would be to move up. I wasn't ready to face the challenge of trying to be the very best. I was afraid of putting in absolutely everything I had and still not coming out on top. That would hurt too much. By not facing up to some of my weaknesses in training I would always have an excuse to fall back on, even though I had had an opportunity to watch other swimmers tackle their weaknesses in my own backyard.

The synchronized swimming team representing Canada at the 1988 Olympics had been chosen early so they would have a full year to practise together and perfect their routines. The team consisted of the duet, Carolyn Waldo and Michelle Cameron, and their alternate, Karin Larsen. They were based in Calgary, so over the year I frequently watched them train.

It was both intriguing and frightening to watch them. They were in the water every day for a minimum of five hours. I was fascinated to see their routines come together. They worked on the most minute details day after day until they perfected small portions of their performance, then they would move on to the next piece of music until they got that right. This continued until they had mastered a four-minute program.

Watching them put together the routine for

the first while was terrifying. What was happening was this: close to a minute of the opening was underwater. The women had to hold their breath while exerting maximum effort to perform their first sequence. When they finally surfaced and took their first breath of air, Michelle would pass out. In the water! Carolyn would be so focused on the music she wouldn't even notice. She just kept on swimming. Debbie Muir, their coach, would say over the microphone, "Carolyn, could you please go back and flip Michelle over?" It was something to see. I can't count the number of times I was ready to dive in and save Michelle.

It is hard to imagine facing that challenge day after day. That is what impressed me about Michelle. She would go back to the pool every day knowing there was a good chance she would pass out, but she persisted. She was determined to work on overcoming this.

It was interesting to see how Debbie Muir handled the situation. If I were a coach and my athletes were passing out, I would probably call 911, but Debbie would just say, "I'll rewind the music and we'll start from there." As soon as Michelle came to, they would try it again. It was the equivalent of getting right back on the horse that throws you.

Eventually Michelle conquered her weakness. She trained herself to withstand the pain and dizziness.

Watching the synchronized swimming team taught me a lot about my own training. It showed me that by taking things one day at a time, one step at a time, you can eventually piece together the entire picture. The four-minute routine seemed impossible to perfect, but by breaking it down into small goals the women were able to master it. It also showed me again what preparing for the Olympics was all about. It wasn't just physical. Michelle's mind refused to accept her body's limitations, and Michelle told herself over and over again that she could do it. And eventually she did.

I was in the stands the day Michelle and Carolyn swam their duet at the Seoul Olympics. Their performance was seemingly effortless, but I knew the work that had gone into it. Years of six-hour days ended with four minutes of perfection. I remembered watching different events on TV as a child and thinking it looked easy. Now I understood why it looked so effortless. Thousands of hours had been invested. There were no short cuts, just a lot of hard work. Maybe that is why people are so emotional when they are victorious. Finally, they realize what the hard work was for. I was overjoyed to see Michelle and Carolyn receive their gold medals.

Another example of persistence in Seoul was Vladimir Salnikov. He had a magnificent career as a swimmer in the Soviet Union. In the 1976 Montreal Olympics, Vladimir competed in the 1500-metre freestyle, the swimmer's equivalent of the marathon. He narrowly missed a medal, coming fourth. He was only sixteen years old, so naturally, he kept competing for four more years to swim in the 1980 Olympics. They were to be held in Moscow, and he would be swimming in front of his own people. At that time, Vladimir had dominated world competition for a number of years and was the favourite to win the Olympic gold medal.

A few months before the Moscow Olympics, President Carter announced that the United States would be boycotting the games because of the Soviet Union's invasion of Afghanistan. Over the course of the following weeks most of the western countries followed the United States' lead and also boycotted. The Olympics were still held, but half of the world was absent. Vladimir Salnikov won his gold medal, but it was not as he had dreamed. He decided to keep swimming for four more years, to try to win when the entire world would be present.

Amazingly, Vladimir continued to dominate the 1500-metre freestyle over those four years. He kept improving and broke his own world record time and time again. He was undefeated in his specialty for more than six years. By the time of the Los Angeles Olympics, in 1984, Vladimir was twenty-four years old, an age at which most swimmers are considered to be at the end of their career, especially in an event like the 1500-metre. Many considered the Los Angeles games in 1984 to be Vladimir's last competition.

A few months before the Olympics were to begin, the Soviet Union announced it would be boycotting the American Olympics for political reasons. The games took place but, like four years earlier, half the world was absent. Vladimir Salnikov did not get his chance after all to win the 1500-metre freestyle with the entire world competing.

In 1986, when I was eighteen, I was representing Canada at the World Championships in Madrid, Spain. I remember being surprised to see Vladimir who was then twenty-six. Thinking he must be coaching, I asked, "Vladimir, what's it like coaching and not swimming?" He looked at me with confusion and replied, "I'm not coaching, I swim still." I was a bit surprised, but thought it was admirable. If anyone could push our sport to new heights, it was Vladimir.

Unfortunately, he didn't have a very good competition. He wasn't even close to winning the event he had dominated for so many years. I felt very badly for him. He had been such a remarkable swimmer but circumstances had prevented him from reaching his ultimate dream.

In 1988, I ran into Vladimir in the Olympic village. This time I didn't make the mistake of assuming he was coaching but waited for him to offer the information first. Much to my dismay, I learned he would be swimming. I felt sorry for this guy. I wanted to say, "Hey, Vladimir, get a life. Give up on this crazy dream." Every time I passed him I looked at him with pity. I couldn't help it. And, of course, Vladimir himself knew that people were saying these things. But like an old warhorse, he kept on going to the site preparing for battle.

Vladimir had one great advantage at these games: nobody was taking him seriously. Everyone was expecting him to fail. His main competitors from Germany and the United States did not consider him a rival. Vladimir had nothing to lose.

On September 24th, the preliminary heats of the 1500-freestyle were swum. In Korea, all eyes

were on Salnikov. He swam one of the best preliminary swims of his life and qualified in second position for the final, to be held the next
day. Because the 1500 is such a gruelling event,
it is the only swim to be held over two consecu-
tive days. This gives the "milers" a day to recover before swimming the final.

There was a transformation in the minds of
many of the Olympic swimmers. After Vladimir's
heat swim he was surrounded by former rivals.
They were all congratulating him and wishing
him the best of luck. In my own mind, I still
didn't really think Vladimir would win the following evening. He was twenty-eight years old
and it would be a lot harder for him to recover
than the younger swimmers he was competing
against. I was very proud of him, though. Even
if he didn't win, he showed us the character of a
champion.

Twenty-four hours later, with over half of the
1500-metre final completed, Vladimir Salnikov
was winning the race. When there were only a
couple of minutes left, all we could hear was a
clapping chant. It was three claps combined
with the sound SAL-NI-KOV, SAL-NI-KOV,
repeated over and over.

A little more than fifteen minutes after the
start of the race, Vladimir Salnikov became one

of the oldest gold medallists in swimming, winning the 1500-metre freestyle at his third Olympic Games. It was one of the greatest moments in our sport's history. The crowd was ecstatic. Salnikov had finally won his Olympic gold medal with the entire world present.

Later that night I was walking behind him as he entered the Olympic cafeteria. The building suddenly grew quiet and all the people—athletes, coaches, delegates alike—burst into applause. Everyone stood up, shouting, "Bravo, Salnikov!" I saw Vladimir try to speak, but as he went to open his mouth his throat tightened and he started crying tears of joy. It was one of the most moving things I have ever seen. These were not just swimmers standing for Vladimir, but all the different athletes from the various Olympic sports and countries paying tribute to a true champion.

A week earlier there had been a consensus that Salnikov would never be able to do it. Everybody agreed except for one person, Salnikov himself. He taught me about persisting and believing in yourself, even when nobody else does.

PATIENCE IS A VIRTUE

As I started working towards my goals again after the 1988 Olympics, I carried with me the lessons I had learned at the games. I knew if I wanted to win the 1992 Olympics I would have to begin training for that now. I knew there would be challenges, maybe right until the moment of victory, but that was what would make the end result all the more satisfying.

My first year back, 1989, proved to be extremely difficult. I had worked harder than I ever had before and I found myself to be ranked only ninth in the world. This was my lowest placing in more than five years. I found myself confronting a professional crisis. Did I have the strength to pull myself out of this all-time low, or should I give up? When I was finally able to look at the year objectively I realized that by training with the national team I had subjected myself to a gruelling, experimental, high-altitude training program. This was a normal procedure for two of the most successful, foreign swim teams in the world at that time. We thought that by duplicating their training methods exactly we could obtain the same outstanding results. We didn't realize, however, that this training program more than likely included the use of performance-enhancing drugs. Of course, this was out of the question for us, and, as a result, we were severely overtrained.

I understood that although in many ways this

had been a worthwhile experiment, it would take me some time to recover physically. My poor world placing was discouraging, but I understood what had caused it. Once I knew what had gone wrong, I could begin to fix it. I took a six-week break to recover from training, and when I felt ready, I came back to the pool and started over.

With time it became apparent that the altitude training, which had been such a gruelling physical experience, turned out to have some long-term benefits. Instead of the immediate results we had hoped for, we found over time it greatly helped our fitness levels. During the next two years I became stronger at finishing my races and slowly regained my position in the world rankings. I eventually found myself in second place. This is where I was, going into the World Championships in Perth, Australia.

The championships started on January 3rd, 1991. I was to compete on the second-last day, January 12th. I watched every race, but stayed a bit removed in order to save my energy for my own performance.

I woke up on the day of the 100-metre backstroke filled with anxiety. This was finally my chance to win an individual medal at a major competition. I went to the pool and forced myself to concentrate on the upcoming race. I knew I had to swim well in the morning so I would be in the right frame of mind for the evening final. After all the results came in, I was ranked second. Jeff Rouse, the American who was ranked first in the world, was over a half-second ahead of me. Things looked very good for a medal that evening, but I realized I would be swimming for a silver.

I went back to the pool that night and prepared for the final. As I jumped into the water for my pre-race warm-up, a sense of calm came over me. I knew I was ready. I swam back and forth for twenty minutes, mainly doing freestyle, and let my mind go blank. After the swimming part of my warm-up was completed, I put on my Walkman and listened to music while stretching out my muscles. I also shut my eyes and visualized the race over and over again. I started to get both my mind and my body into a state ready to compete. My actual race took less than a minute to complete but my pre-race preparation lasted more than two hours.

With a half-hour to go it was time to check into the ready room. I was feeling perfectly prepared and surprisingly unafraid. My two main competitors would be Rouse, the American, and a Spaniard, Martin Lopez-Zubero. In the ready room I could sense many of my competitors observing me. This was a great omen because I knew if my competitors were watching me they wouldn't be concentrating on themselves. Rouse was lying on the floor immediately outside the room shaking out. Lopez-Zubero came over to me and said, "Rouse looks really nervous tonight. I think you can beat him. I think you can win." I smiled, not because he thought I could beat Rouse but because I was just as worried about beating Zubero. By telling me this, he was practically throwing in the white towel. The chief marshal came in and lined us up for the march out to the pool. It was time to race.

As we were standing waiting to march out it was very quiet. Nobody was speaking, we were all just taking deep breaths to calm our nerves. In the distance I heard the announcer say "Ladies and gentlemen, please welcome the finalists for the men's 100-metre backstroke" and we started off. We came out at the halfway point of the pool and had to walk 25 metres to the starting end. As we entered the open air of the outdoor pool I heard this incredible roar. It was the Canadian team cheering. I felt a massive adrenaline rush and had to tell myself to calm down because my fingers and toes were tingling. A band was playing; the Australian military saluted as we walked by. This was it.

The introductions went quickly. Before I knew it we were in the water waiting for the start of the race. I heard the gun and shot off the wall. I was in lane five, Rouse was on one side of me in lane four, and a Russian was in lane six. After the start I was ahead of the Russian but I knew I was behind Rouse. At the halfway point I was feeling good but had no sense of where I was in relation to Rouse. I did a turn and the most remarkable thing happened. For years the turn was one of my greatest weaknesses. I had worked on this part of my race relentlessly in the training camps trying to perfect it. On the evening of my final I mastered it and had the best turn of my life. As I started on the second length I could sense someone beside me. With 25 metres to go I could see Jeff out of the corner of my eye. We were together stroke for stroke. We stayed in this position for all of the last 25 metres.

As I hit the wall I turned around and looked up at the scoreboard. I found my name and looked at the results. It said

TEWKSBURY, MARK   CAN   55.29   2.

I had won the silver medal. I was excited but I had to see who had won. I looked and it read

ROUSE, JEFF   USA   55.23   1.

Jeff had won the race by 6/100ths of a second. It was that close. I was very proud even though I had missed becoming world champion by fractions. I felt content because I had done everything possible to prepare for this race. It came down to not being afraid to win. And I wasn't. On this day someone was a little better than I was and I could live with that. This time I hadn't beaten myself.

I had risen to the challenge.

ONE STEP FORWARD, THREE STEPS BACK

The World Championships set the stage for my Olympic preparation. Since I had come so close to winning, I figured my training program was obviously working. For the rest of the year I continued the same type of preparation I had used in getting ready for the Worlds.

Later that year, in August of 1991, I swam in the Pan Pacific Championships, which were held in Edmonton. Since I hadn't done anything differently, I figured I would again be close to Jeff and could even take over the number one spot in the world rankings. I was gravely mistaken.

While I had carried on training in a similar way, my competition around the world had improved significantly. I swam a personal best that summer with a time of 55.19. The only problem was that Jeff Rouse also swam a best time. His was not only a personal best but also the best time achieved in the history of the event. He became the world record holder with a time of 53.93.

In my dreams I thought it might be possible for me to swim a time of 54.50. That was an outrageous, wild dream that I kept in my head, but now I had to deal with the reality that one of my competitors had made an enormous breakthrough and swum my event in 53.93 seconds. 53.93! I was over 1.2 seconds behind him. During all my years of swimming I had dreamed of winning the Olympic gold medal but this now seemed impossible. From the time I was sixteen until the summer of 1991, when I was twenty-three, I had improved a total of 1.2 seconds. Now I had to make that same pro-gression in less than a year. How could I ever do it?

In September, as I started back into my training program, I found myself facing one of the biggest challenges of my career. I would be working towards winning the Olympic gold medal feeling a bit like Vladimir Salnikov had in 1988, when nobody believed he could do it. I knew this year would be full of demands and I would have to persevere through them. There was an almost insurmountable quantity of work that needed to be completed.

Michelle and Vladimir had both shown me what the mind could do in training. What I had to achieve seemed impossible, yet they, too, had faced incredible odds. Where did they find their motivation, and where, in turn, would I find mine?

SUMMARY

Persisting Through Challenges

Never give up.

Believe in yourself, even when nobody else does.

Sometimes you need to fail before you can succeed.

If the mind believes it, the body can achieve it.

"There are no shortcuts to any place worth going."
BEVERLY SILLS

Mum,
Dad
and
me,
1968

With
Dad,
1972

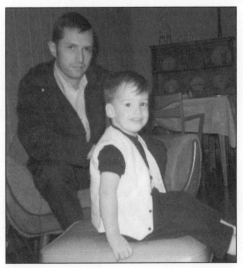

With my brother Scott and sister
Colleen, Dallas, 1974

At the
pool in
Dallas

In grade 6

Showing off my trophies in 1980

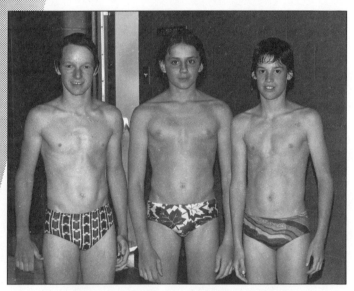

With Bernie Giesen (left) and Gabriel
Brovadani (centre) at Canyon Meadows
swimming pool, Calgary

4

Living With Passion

"Remember that what pulls the strings
is the force hidden within;
there lies the power..."
MARCUS AURELIUS

FRANK KING, HEAD OF THE ORGANIZING Committee for the Calgary Olympics, once told me a story about something that happened in one of the volunteer meetings. After the games were over, he asked people to share their favourite memories of the experience. An elderly woman rose and told him nobody in her life had ever asked her to give this much before. She had to demand more of herself to help carry off such an enormous event. She then thanked Frank for the challenge.

When I heard this story I realized that I was in a similar situation. When your expectations are high you strive harder to meet them.

It all comes back to a cycle I have experienced over the years. When I was a kid this is what happened: I took the first step by starting swimming; this was the action. As I became involved in the program, I entered a second stage in which my actions became motivated by external rewards. These compensations varied over time but there was always something to work for. As time passed this external motivation changed, which was the third step. I became motivated internally, no longer needing rewards of material value. I was inspired to work because I loved what I was doing. Finally, this love of my "work" was fed by an underlying passion which fuelled my expectations. The more I loved what I was doing, the greater my expectations were. This provided added motivation which brought me back to the actions. Because my motivation was high my actions improved. The cycle looked something like this: Action—External Motivation—Internal Motivation/Passion—Higher Level of Action. Once started, the action would improve only if there was some incentive.

BECOMING MOTIVATED

Where did the motivation come from? It started when I was very young. There may have been internal motivation but I didn't recognize it at the time. When I was eight years old I had coaches who really understood how to externally motivate kids. Every Friday night we would have "chocolate bar" races. At that age I wasn't interested in certificates or ribbons, but I was certainly interested in those chocolate bars. I raced my heart out to try to win. I went after it with everything I had.

The chocolate bars eventually led to ice cream. Every year there was an enormous swim meet for kids aged ten to fourteen called the Hyack Invitational, held in Vancouver. For every best time we swam, our coach, Larry Nielsen, would reward us with an ice cream cone. If we achieved three best times, we could upgrade to a sundae. Five best times and we could go for the big treats—banana splits and sundae supremes. I went up and ordered a banana split, which was fine, but then I ordered a sundae as well. Mr. Nielsen looked at me disapprovingly but I reminded him that I had set eight best times. That worked out to exactly what I was ordering. Besides, I pointed to my mother and explained that she would be receiving the sundae. All Mr. Nielsen could do was laugh.

The chocolate and ice cream were simple, fun rewards. They gave me something to work for that I wanted. But somewhere along the way these treats became secondary. I realized it wasn't the external rewards that were motivating me. My motivation was coming from within. I was passionate about what swimming was doing for me, giving me the opportunity to be a little better at something every day.

I think a lot of people go through life without very much passion because they never find anything they truly love to do. I was fortunate because I loved what I was doing. I couldn't have kept at it for so many years if I hadn't.

In the worlds of sport and public speaking I have had opportunities to meet incredibly successful people. It is difficult to find a common thread in all their personalities but if there is one thing they share, it is a passion for what they are doing. It is obvious when people love what they do. When they talk they literally come alive. Their enthusiasm is infectious, and you can't help but get caught up in the intensity of their feelings.

THE FIRE WITHIN

I was in my teens when the external motivation really began to turn inward. All the material rewards in the world couldn't have motivated me. The emphasis shifted to how I felt about myself. Chocolate bars and ice cream made way for pride and self-respect.

If there were still times when I was driven by force, it was now a person instead of a reward. When my motivation waned I would look up to successful individuals for the impetus to keep me passionate. One of these individuals was Victor Davis.

If there was ever a role model for living with passion, for living life to its fullest, it was Victor. He was rebellious, rough and seemingly undisciplined. He had a wild energy that nobody seemed able to control.

When Victor was in his early teens his father, Mel, enrolled him in a swimming program.

Through sport Victor learned to control some of his energy by directing it towards one goal. He was able to focus on something constructive every day when he went to swimming practice.

I remember first hearing about Victor when I was fourteen years old. I was swimming in a big youth competition in Winnipeg and an announcement was made that Victor Davis had just won the 100-metre breaststroke at the World Championships in Guayaquil, Equador.

In March of the following year, 1983, I swam in the Canadian National Championships for the first time. I was just a young kid, barely fifteen years old, and I was in total awe the entire time I was there. I will never forget my first sight of Victor Davis; his intensity was awesome. He didn't just jump in and swim; it was a big production. He leapt up and down and splashed himself and spat water out and had everybody's attention. What struck me the most was the fire in his eyes. When Victor was about to swim, or even when he just walked into a room, you noticed. He had this incredible energy about him that was totally electrifying.

When I finally made the national team in 1985, Victor was then twenty-one, and still at his prime in the swimming world. Although we swam together in international competitions for three years, I was intimidated by him for a long time.

It wasn't really until 1988 at the Seoul Olympics that Victor and I became close. In his individual race, the 100-metre breaststroke, he came fourth. In my own race I was fifth, so I think Vic could empathize with me. On the last day of the games we teamed up together with two other swimmers and formed the medley relay.

Strange as it may seem, the relay never trains together. Because the four swimmers are chosen from the results of the competition, it is impossible to say exactly who will be on the team. It isn't decided until the night before the race.

When our team for Seoul was assembled, people thought we would come fourth or fifth, but our coaches thought we had a chance at a bronze medal. Until this race the men's team hadn't won a single medal at these Olympics. It would be the last chance for any of us at these games.

On race day the relay team spent more than twelve hours together. We went down to the pool in the morning and qualified for the final. We ate lunch together in the cafeteria at our own table. Throughout the day we started to believe we were a very special unit. This was no easy feat. Joining Victor and me were Sandy Goss and Tom Ponting. The four of us were about as different as four people could be. But on this one day we put all of our differences aside and came together for the same reason; we all wanted to win a medal.

The real backbone of the group was Victor. Whenever there was a quiet time Vic would say softly that he thought we could do it. He said that on paper it looked as if we should come fourth or maybe third, but he really thought we could win a silver medal if we had the race of our lives. The look in his eyes and the tone of his voice were so intense I had to believe him.

We all went our separate ways for a rest after the heats, but we met together in the cafeteria for a light meal before going to the pool for the final. We only talked of winning. That day the fire wasn't just in Victor's eyes, we all shared some of that spark.

The magic started to happen during the warm-up. There are always two pools at the Olympics, one for training, one for the competition. Until finals begin many athletes use the competition pool for their last preparations. The feeling becomes electric as race time approaches. The television lights are turned on, journalists and photographers begin running around, the stands start to fill up with spectators. Instead of swimming during this time, the four of us sat on the deck stretching and watching the activity in the pool. As we sat there the feeling in the building began to charge us. By the time warm-up was over I felt energized.

We went into the training pool area and from this moment on we didn't leave each other. We didn't want to lose the collective energy that Victor's intensity had created.

Thirty minutes before the race we went into the ready room and sat together. It was a crowded area before the relay because instead of just eight men in there for the final, there were thirty-two of the world's best swimmers. I wanted to look around and see who was present, but every time I looked up, Victor would grab my head and pull it back down so I would have to look at the floor. Every few minutes he would look me in the eyes and ask if I was ready. I would nod and he would ask louder, "Are you ready?" I would say "Yes, Victor." I didn't want to let him down.

Before the race the chief marshal came in and started to line us up for the march onto the pool deck. We qualified in lane three, in between the US and USSR. I led the Canadian team, followed by Victor, Tom and Sandy. This would be the order in which we would swim the race. As we started to march out, Victor asked me for the last time if I was ready. I nodded; this time I was.

I swam the first leg of the relay and had a respectable swim. We were in fourth place but were within striking distance of the Russians beside us, who were the silver medal favourites. Victor swam the next leg and had the race of his life. He moved our team from fourth to third and was only a few tenths of a second behind the Soviets. With the US in the lead it became clear that it was going to be a race between Canada and the USSR for the silver and bronze medals. Tom had a great swim in the butterfly leg and stayed in virtually the same position Victor had put us in. It all came down to our last swimmer, Sandy Goss.

The man swimming the freestyle anchor leg for the Russians was better than Sandy. If you compared their best times, Sandy was half a second behind. We knew it and the Russians knew it. I was standing behind the blocks with Victor and we were yelling at Sandy as he was getting to ready to dive in. Victor was going crazy, yelling and screaming at Sandy to go like hell, telling him we could beat the Russians but it was all up to him. Tom hit the wall and Sandy took off.

He was on fire. He stayed with the Russian Genvad Progoda for the first length and started to catch him on the second part of the race. The crowds in the stands were on their feet going absolutely berserk. The race was so close. Victor, Tom and I were all standing on the pool deck screaming. The officials pushed us aside but Victor pushed right back so he could stay and cheer Sandy on. He jumped up on the block, while I stood at his side and screamed for Sandy to hit the wall.

As he hit, we looked up at the scoreboard and saw that the number two was beside Canada. We were ecstatic. Victor, Tom and I almost dove in the water to hug Sandy. We were jumping up and down like fools, hugging each other on the pool deck for a long time until the results were made official. We had won the silver medal.

I had never been part of an Olympic medal ceremony, so I kept watching Victor, who had been through this before. He glowed that evening. Victor had produced the swim of his life when we needed it the most. He had been a gold medallist four years earlier in Los Angeles, but he told journalists that this silver meant even more to him than the gold medal had. For this one, he said, he had to find the fire within.

I felt very much like Victor that evening. I had discovered how to push the limits. Our relay team had passionately gone after something that many people felt was impossible and we had come out ahead. I shared in the relay's passion and in doing so became ignited myself. The four of us, who had never really been close before, would always share something special. We overcame our own barriers and united to give this effort everything we had. Something changed in me that night. I had never felt as high as I did after the medal ceremony.

In the spring of 1989, Victor retired from swimming. I wasn't surprised. After all, he had been through two Olympics and had basically accomplished everything a swimmer could aspire to, but I was saddened. I would miss Victor on the national team. His spirit and energy were truly rare.

On November 11th, I was out running errands most of the day. When I came home there were many messages on my answering machine from people I would never expect to hear from at this time of year. Carolyn Waldo had called from Toronto to see how I was doing. Reporters from *The Toronto Sun* and *The Toronto Star* had called to talk to me. Michelle Cameron had also phoned. I remember thinking how odd it was that everyone was calling at the same time. Something just didn't seem right. Finally there was a message from my mother and father asking if I was okay. They had just heard "the news about Victor."

I had no idea what was going on but soon learned that Victor had been involved in a very serious hit-and-run accident and was in very bad shape in a hospital in Montreal. I was shocked. For a day I didn't know how bad things really were but then I was told that Victor was in a coma and the chances of his recovering were almost nil. I felt sick and numb. This couldn't possibly be happening. It didn't seem real.

Two days later, at the age of twenty-five, Victor Davis died. He had been so full of life, so passionate, so seemingly invincible. To have lost him at such an early age wasn't fair. I watched the memorials and tributes on TV and there he was, larger than life, winning the Olympics or breaking a world record. Victor had inspired me and shared in one of the greatest days of my life and now he was gone. For a while it felt as if all my passion had gone with him.

His parents asked me to be one of the pallbearers at the funeral. All of the relay team from Seoul, as well as fellow swimmers Alex Baumann, Mike West and Vlastimil Cerny, were pallbearers. We wore Canadian track-suit jackets with large maple leaf emblems for Victor. It was a really hard day. So many old friends had come together but for such a tragic reason.

I remember Alex looking absolutely blank. Of all of us he was probably the closest to Victor. They had both been on top of the world at the same time. But Alex was being so strong. I think if he had broken down everybody would have followed. Victor's family was astonishing, too. Mel, Vic's father, somehow had the strength to find humour on this day. We shared stories about Victor before going to the church and after every story you had to smile and say, "Oh, that was Victor!"

One of the hardest parts of the day for me was the ride to the church. We followed the hearse in a procession to the service. On the street, lining the way, were Royal Canadian Mounted Police in uniform. They were saluting as we drove by. One of the officers had tears streaming down his face as we passed him. It made me start to cry.

Sitting in the church, surrounded by friends and family of Victor, I felt somehow peaceful. It was sad. We were saying goodbye, but we were strong. The priest focused on uplifting things and gave a beautiful sermon. Victor was so full of life and had brought joy to many people. He hadn't lived life as if he was waiting for it to happen. He attacked it, lived every day as if it was the most important.

I had always thought that life would start for me after my swimming career was completed. Real life, that is, the day-to-day things I was missing, like getting a job, having a relationship, spending time with family and friends. I had watched Victor start on his new path with excitement. He'd started a new business and had big plans. And now he was gone.

Victor's death was a wake-up call for me. Life becomes more precious when you realize there is less of it to waste.

REKINDLING THE FIRE

In the months following the funeral I did change for a while. I lived with passion, took chances, became more of a team leader. But with time, as the grief and pain faded, so did my intensity. I fell back into my old habits of taking things for granted. My desire to succeed wasn't as urgent.

In 1991, as I was getting ready for the Olympics, once again I heard those wake-up calls. The first came in June, in Calgary, at a dinner held at Canada Olympic Park. The purpose of the evening was to induct the 1960 Winter Olympic Champions into the hall of fame. It was a special night because many Olympians came to honour their peers. In the same room were more than a hundred Olympians representing fifty years of competition. I was very proud to be there.

The highlight of the evening for me came when all the inductees spoke. My favourite was Nancy Greene Raine. She spoke about how special it had been to be a part of the Olympics. As a rookie she had shared a room in 1960 with skier Anne Heggtveit and watched her win. Seeing the congratulatory telegrams and sharing her excitement rekindled her own dream. She remembered expecting Anne to be different in some way and being surprised she wasn't. She washed her socks in the same sink, woke up in the morning and brushed her teeth, just like everybody else. What made all the difference to Nancy was that she had seen her win, and by seeing how normal Anne was, Nancy could imagine doing it herself.

She spoke of this from the heart and with passion. It made me think of my own heroes, watching the Olympics and then, years later, seeing Alex Baumann and Victor Davis doing what I had dreamed about. I understood what Nancy was speaking of. Through the following months whenever I needed inspiration I thought of her speech. It revived my passion and increased my expectations of myself, which enabled me to work towards a higher level.

MAKING THE FLAME BURN BRIGHTER

Six months later, in December of 1991, my swimming team travelled to Australia to train in an environment that would simulate conditions in Barcelona. The men were to stay in a surfing club, which sounded glamorous, until we arrived. There was no air conditioning, roaches and fleas were everywhere, and there were forty people bunking in the room, with absolutely no privacy. The average temperature was 35 degrees Celsius. The bugs were so bad that before going to bed we would all have to spray each other down with insect repellant, and then halfway through the night we would wake up and respray so we wouldn't be eaten alive. It was incredibly tough to live like this and work around the clock for more than three weeks.

We swam twice a day. The pool was a five-kilometre bike ride each way. We would wake up at five in the morning, cycle to the pool and then swim for three hours. In the afternoon we swam from one until four, in the most scorching heat of the day. It didn't matter how much protection you put on your skin, it would eventually wash off. We were sunburned, training harder than ever, and living in horrible conditions. Why were we doing this?

The answer was simple. Seven months later we would travel to Barcelona and share rooms with ten other people. There would be no air conditioning and it would be as hot as it was in Australia. By experiencing these conditions now, we would be better able to face the village in Barcelona.

At times I seriously questioned if all of this was worth it. I wanted to be prepared as best I could but my passion was waning. I wasn't as motivated as I needed to be to benefit from this period. And then I received another wake-up call.

While we were there we spent some of the workouts training with an Australian coach, Laurie Lawrence. Laurie has a reputation of being a madman. We found out why.

He set up workouts in which his group would swim head to head against ours. It became more than just a team against a team, it became Canada against Australia. The workout consisted of one main component called a heart-rate set. For four thousand metres, which is a hundred and sixty lengths, approximately one hour of swimming time, the goal was to keep your heart rate over 180 beats per minute. We would swim for approximately sixty seconds all out and then have a break for twenty seconds. In that break a coach would take our pulse to make sure we were working as hard as we could. It was like nothing I had ever done before.

The first time we did this set was at a morning workout. We bicycled to the pool at 5:00 A.M., changed and went out on the pool deck and heard the instructions one last time. Laurie was very animated. He was screaming and telling us to get someone to challenge. He wanted to see who was going to last the longest in the set. At this stage I was so nervous I felt sick to my stomach.

We did a warm-up, moved into our respective lanes and then the set began. After the first seven minutes my body started to go numb and I couldn't really feel my legs any more. After fifteen minutes the pain was so great I didn't know if I could stand it much longer. Every time I came to the end of a length I swore.

After twenty minutes the pain was numbing. For the next forty-five minutes the goal was to hang on and keep your heart rate up. I had to learn to cope with this pain because it's the same feeling I experience in the last stretch of a race.

Every time I came to the end of the pool Laurie was standing there yelling words of encouragement at me, and telling everybody what a great job I was doing. I didn't want to disappoint him so I kept going. My times slowed down but my heart rate was always over 180. And Laurie was always there waiting for me. His energy sustained me. He wouldn't let me give up. Even when I was pleading to stop, he kept yelling at me to be tough and stick to it. With his help I made it through the set.

The first thing I did upon finishing was to throw up. I couldn't control the pain. The workout was only half-completed, so I knew I still had to get back in and swim. When it was finally over I was overcome with pride that we had made it through this challenge. I felt dead tired yet full of life. Laurie told me how impressed he was and that he thought I could win in Barcelona this summer. I was certainly tough enough, he said, and it was a pleasure to watch me train. This was coming from a man who had coached two unknown swimmers to gold in the past two Olympics. I knew you didn't earn his respect easily. His words meant a great deal to me.

At this stage I still doubted myself very much, so it was important that people like Laurie gave me support. It helped me believe in myself when someone with so much passion endorsed my efforts.

After Australia my expectations rose again. I was reminded of the elderly volunteer Frank King had told me about. I asked myself to be that good for the period before the games. I heard the wake-up call and knew, with less than seven months to go, there was no time to waste.

Throughout the year I was continually going through cycles. One day I would be on top of the world and think my training was right on track and the next day I would feel as if everything I did was useless and I would never win. My actions changed according to my feelings. Some days I would be fuelled by fear, others I was carried along by the belief I could do it. Through it all I remained motivated. By the time I was into the final stages of my preparation I had come through Victor's death, I had heard Nancy speak, and I had seen Laurie's excitement over my potential. Each one of these experiences raised my internal motivation, which led to an ever-rising expectation level which I passionately attempted to sustain. I really wanted to be the Olympic champion.

SUMMARY

Staying Motivated

Live with passion.

Take your wake-up calls.

Keep your expectations high.

Take the appropriate actions
to meet your expectations.

"Choose a job you love, and you will
never have to work a day in your life."
CONFUCIUS

5

Who's in Control
Here, Anyway?

"Your past is not your potential.
In any hour you can choose to
liberate the future."
MARILYN FERGUSON

I F YOU ARE GOING TO LIVE WITH PASSION AND enthusiasm you have to learn to assume a certain amount of responsibility for your actions, and sometimes that means going your own way.

When I was growing up I had two sets of guardians, at home my mother and father and at the pool my coach. My parents encouraged me to make my own decisions and deal with the consequences. When I was seventeen I started doing a lot of international travelling. I would dread coming home because I felt so free on the road and coming back to my parents' house made me feel restricted. I decided I wanted to move out. I knew my mother and father weren't too enthusiastic about the idea but they let me do it anyway, on one condition. Once I was out I had to stay out for at least a year. If things didn't go as I had planned I couldn't just come back home. I was to be responsible for my actions. Of course, living on my own wasn't everything I had dreamed of. There were times when I wanted to go running back, but I abided by the arrangement. It was through lessons like this that I gradually became more independent.

At the pool, the situation was different. The communication between my coaches and me was all one-way. They talked and I listened. At first this made perfect sense. After all, they were the experts, I was the beginner. For years I followed blindly without questioning. There comes a point, though, when any serious athlete knows enough about their sport and themselves to take a more active role in their own development. This is when a good coach begins to listen as well as instruct, and communication starts to flow both ways.

As the years passed I started to get a feel for the purpose behind our actions—I understood why the coach was asking us to do certain things. By the time I was eighteen and swimming on the national team I had a really good understanding of what worked and what didn't for me. But I was never able to communicate this to my coach, Deryk Snelling.

Deryk is a very knowledgeable man, active in the sport of swimming for more than forty years, and I had swum with him since I was fourteen years old. I credit him with taking me on as an inexperienced, hyper-active youth and training me, motivating me, and pushing me until I could compete on an international level. It is largely thanks to Deryk that I made it.

Any long-lasting relationship between coach and athlete is bound to be intense. Both spend years focusing on the ultimate goal of developing the athlete's skills, physique and performance until the athlete functions like a perfectly tuned machine. But, of course, the athlete isn't a machine and egos and emotions inevitably surface. A good coach not only gives technical advice but also probes and pushes the athlete beyond the comfort zone. Through the process, an intense love-hate relationship can develop. The athlete loves the coach for putting everything he has into providing the skills and development needed to get to the top, but naturally resents being forced to perform beyond what seems humanly possible.

There came a time in my relationship with Deryk when I was convinced I needed training in a specific area that he didn't agree with. Our relationship was so intense and our communication so one-way that when I suggested spending time on it, and Deryk dismissed it, I couldn't bring myself to stand up for what I believed. For the time being I dropped it.

Luckily, in spite of our communication problems, 95 per cent of the time Deryk was right. But I was still frustrated because I wanted to have some control. I wanted to actively participate in my own future, and what seemed like a small failure in our communication would come back later to haunt us.

JUST LISTEN

In 1987, I was ranked second in the world leading into the Olympic year. I thought I could win my Olympic medal in the 100-metre backstroke, and then take a more active role in my own training. Just one more year and my situation would improve.

In the fall, less than a year before the Olympics, life threw me a curve ball. Swimmers around the world began doing a new start and turn. They were swimming the underwater dolphin kick off the start and again off the turn for great distances. Some guys were swimming forty-five out of a possible fifty metres underwater, turning and doing it again. The results were stunning, because it is possible to swim faster underwater than on the surface. Swimmers I had never heard of were suddenly ahead of me in the world rankings. I moved from second to seventh in a matter of a few months. It was a terrible time for me.

I desperately tried to learn this underwater kick, but it was really hard for me. My strength has always been my sheer swimming speed. I have never been particularly good at the technical aspects of my sport, such as the start and turn. Just wind me up, put me in the water and watch me go like hell.

When I tried the new underwater kick, my team-mates would cringe. I would start in lane four, with everybody watching me, push off and start down the length. I would kick as hard as I could until I started to feel faint and water was coming up my nose, then I would stop. I always ended up on the other side of the pool, in lane eight. It was a disaster.

I saw my dream disappearing. This was not backstroke any more. This was underwater racing. To me the rules were never meant to be interpreted this way.

For a few months it seemed like every time I came to the pool there was news about another breakthrough for a swimmer in the 100-metre backstroke. The world record was getting faster and faster, and I was being left further and further behind. I felt it was crucial for me to try to learn this new technique. The competition was improving so dramatically that I was becoming obsolete. I believed I wouldn't have a chance at the Olympics unless I learned this start.

During this whole period Deryk and I were having our usual communication problems. He didn't acknowledge my working on the underwater start for a long time. Eventually, however, he told me two things. First, I was a terrible underwater kicker, and second, I should work on my strengths instead of focusing on my weaknesses. I could outswim my competitors if I got to the surface of the water quickly off the start. My strength lay in my speed.

I knew he was right about my speed. He may have been right about focusing on my strengths, but because he never worked with me on the underwater start, I couldn't accept his word.

The Olympic year turned into a constant struggle for me. I was so disappointed in Deryk for ignoring the underwater start that I started to lose faith in him in other areas. I would listen to what he was saying but in my mind I thought he was wrong. I felt as though he wasn't giving me a chance. I thought the only reason he didn't want to help me on the underwater start was because he didn't understand it himself. The closer we got to the games the more hopeless I felt.

I think one of the reasons I had so much trouble in Seoul was that I felt stranded. I wasn't strong enough yet to believe my plan was right but I also didn't believe Deryk's was. Consequently, I had no plan.

I remember sitting in the ready room before the final of the 1988 Olympics and I couldn't focus. I literally didn't know if I was going to swim underwater or just as usual. Here I was, minutes before my dream final, and I had absolutely no idea what to do. I ended up compromising. I didn't go nearly as far underwater as the true kickers but I didn't start swimming right away either. I never once thought I was going to win the race. I couldn't even decide how I was going to swim it, let alone think about winning. As a result, I came a disappointing fifth.

After the Olympics I felt very angry. I was mad at myself for not taking control. By this time in my life it was ultimately my responsibility to get ready and create a competitive plan. I had failed in doing that.

I learned from Seoul that I could never let anybody decide my fate for me. I had to be a part of the plan and have a say in the process. Not only that, I would have to learn to communicate with the people around me if I was ever going to make real progress. Had Deryk and I been able to communicate better we would have had the strength of our combined knowledge instead of two separate energies fighting each other for the same goal.

CHANGING OF THE GUARD

If I was going to swim for four more years I wanted to take control. I didn't want to go through this experience again and feel as though I hadn't done everything possible because I was too afraid to communicate with the boss. It was time to become more independent.

This was easier said than done. Swimming is an individual sport but we trained together as a team. I swam with a minimum of fourteen other swimmers. Individuality in practice was often sacrificed for the good of the group as a whole. It was very hard to work for six hours a day by yourself and really be pushed to the limits. That was one of the purposes of the team. Whenever you were tired there was always someone there challenging you and keeping you going.

Deryk was a great team builder, unquestionably one of the best. But there were only so many hours in the day, and it was impossible for him to give everybody the individual attention they needed in order to take them to the top. I stopped waiting for things to be done and started working on them myself. I became selfish. I decided I shouldn't keep doing what was right for the team if it wasn't right for me. It was time to start listening to my own instincts.

It wasn't a radical change. I just started to pick and choose a little more. I learned to prioritize what was important for me in the workouts and what wasn't. If there was a set that was stroke specific, meaning I would work my back-stroke, I gave it everything I had. If the set was a long freestyle set, which was used for base training, I would work it but I wouldn't give it 100 per cent. I was taking control of my training program.

At first I doubted some of my decisions. For years I had been told what to do, so it took a while for me to gain the self-confidence to make my own choices. When my results in racing reinforced my efforts, I started to take a bit more liberty in the decision-making process. I started to not only change the structure of the workouts to fit my own needs, but also to work outside the program on things I thought needed some help. I did supplementary weight training and extra stroke work. I also made some "executive" decisions. If I was exhausted and thought the best thing for me was to get some extra rest, I slept in. I never missed a crucial workout but if sleeping was going to do me more good than practising, I slept.

Deryk could see that something was changing in me because I started standing up for myself. If he said something I really disagreed with, I let him know. It didn't happen often, but if I was pushed enough I would speak up. I was starting to shift the control and becoming responsible for my actions.

DÉJÀ VU

In 1991, when I looked at the upcoming year I realized I had major work to do in some areas. After Seoul the rules for the 100-metre back-stroke changed. The international swimming body, Federation Internationale Natation Amateur, changed the rules the day after the Seoul Olympics. Swimmers now had to surface from the start and the turn within fifteen metres. This was great for me, because of my swimming speed, but I still had to contend with some underwater swimming. My competitors, even after only fifteen metres, were so far ahead off the start that I really didn't have a chance. I would have to work on the underwater if I were to have a serious shot at the Olympics.

I knew this was going to cause some prob-lems. In four years Deryk and I still had not worked on this together. With less than a year to go I knew there was no time left. We would have to begin working on the start immediately.

September came and went and nothing hap-pened. Deryk, once again, didn't think the underwater was the answer and I didn't know how to approach the issue without having a repeat performance of 1988. I decided that it was time I started to create some of my own opportunities. At the risk of upsetting a lot of people, I went outside the circle of speed swimming and did what any business person would do. I hired a consultant.

After watching Carolyn and Michelle train in 1988, I remembered how great their coach, Debbie Muir, was at technical things. She is very analytical and is also brilliant at underwater training. In her it seemed I had found my answer, unconventional though it might be. Synchronized swimming is sometimes dismissed as less physically challenging but I knew this wasn't true. Even though no other speed swimmer I knew had ever gone to a synchro coach, I thought I could benefit from Debbie's expertise.

I met with Debbie and she was excited about the idea of helping me. There was only one concern. She wanted to make sure it was acceptable to Deryk. That was going to be up to me. One of the hardest things I've ever had to do was sit down with Deryk and explain the situation to him. I didn't want to insult him by going outside the system but at the same time I couldn't procrastinate.

When the opportunity came, after I had swum particularly well in a workout, I approached Deryk. I explained that I thought I should work on my start a little more, making it clear that I wasn't obsessed with it, but 30 per cent of my race could still be swum underwater. It took a while but he saw my point. Then came the hard part. When he asked what we were going to do about it, I said I wanted to get some outside help because we'd been in this situation before and nothing had happened. I pointed out that there were fourteen of us in our group working towards going to the Olympics this year, and it would be impossible for him to give me the attention I needed.

I suggested Debbie's name and let him think about it for a while. It may not seem like much but I had taken a giant leap in my Olympic preparation.

Deryk, Debbie and I never did sit down as a group to discuss the plan for the underwater kick. Deryk knew I was working with her but it was never really talked about, and that was fine. The important thing was that I was working on that damn kick.

When Debbie and I started, we put together a routine full of drills and strengthening exercises to make the kick better. Every Tuesday and Thursday when I was finished with my usual swimming workout, I would work with Debbie for an hour when no one else was around. The progress was painstakingly slow but after a few months I began to improve. I became more comfortable with the drills, to the point where I could start to incorporate them into my normal swimming practice without anyone noticing.

The year was a long one, because although we thought my kick was getting better, it was hard to truly measure it. I was doing well in Canada but until I raced the other top-ranked swimmers in the world I wouldn't know for sure. This wouldn't happen until the Olympics. The most important thing for me was that I *thought* the kick was getting better. Whether it was or not became almost irrelevant. I felt better because we were working on it. And it certainly wasn't getting any worse.

BREAKDOWNS CAUSE BREAKTHROUGHS

In March of 1992, the Winter Olympics were over and the sporting world turned its attention to the Summer Olympians. It was my turn next and I felt a sense of panic. There were only four months left, and I knew the time had come for Deryk and me to really talk.

My breakthrough with Deryk finally came at a camp in New Mexico, where we had gone for two weeks of high-altitude training. Swimming at a high altitude is very difficult. The first day it feels as though you are going to die. It is hard to even swim a tenth of what you are used to at home, and the lack of oxygen really takes its toll on your system.

Inevitably I got really over-tired there. We started slowly to adjust but built up to a full program, swimming five hours a day, within the first week. By the ninth day I was so exhausted I thought I was going to die. On March 20th we had a workout that was extra challenging. We did a monitored stroke set, which meant that as we were swimming, our results were being compared to past performances. This was at the beginning of workout. When we were done this set I was absolutely wasted but we still had more than an hour left in the practice.

I was a total mess. After a brief shower, I felt disoriented and tried to re-join the workout, but just couldn't seem to get into it. I jumped back into the pool but spent most of the practice clinging to the wall. I did all of this without Deryk noticing—or so I thought.

I went home from workout thinking no more about it. Two hours later I got a phone call. It was Deryk. He wanted to know if anything was wrong with me, if I felt sick or physically hurt or anything. I said no, I felt fine, but wondered why he was asking. Oh, he said, I noticed you missed about half the workout tonight.

I hung up the phone and felt really angry. I

wasn't upset because I was caught missing half the workout; after all, he was right. I was mad because here we were, four months to go before the Olympics, and we still couldn't be up front with each other. If he had asked me at the pool what the hell was wrong I would have explained why I had to miss part of practice. I felt sick. It was the fact that he phoned hours later that upset me. If he thought something was wrong why didn't he ask me at the pool. Or for that matter, why didn't I tell him. I realized we still couldn't communicate openly so I went to see him.

I started by apologizing for missing most of the workout. Then I said, "I think it's time we start communicating with each other. If you don't think I have done my job at the pool, then please let me know. But let me know *at the pool* so we can do something about it. Don't come to me hours after the fact and bring it up. We don't have time to waste workouts any more."

Deryk and I talked for close to an hour. We actually communicated, each of us speaking as well as listening to what the other had to say. It was a great conversation. We talked about the state of my training and what had to be done before the games. He surprised me by saying he actually liked the fact that I had missed part of the workout and he wanted me to start doing what I wanted to do. His main concern was that I wasn't drained by the time I got to the Olympics.

When we talked it became clear that we both had the same goal. That day in March turned out to be an important one for me. I had broken down twice, and although they may not be labelled as big breakdowns, they were significant to me. They forced me to take control and face the problem immediately. In doing so I didn't make things worse, I made a breakthrough.

THE GAME PLAN

For the following months things went well. I was able to talk to Deryk about my training and I felt I was being heard. For the first time we were talking and working as partners.

In May I left Canada for the final preparation phase heading into the Olympics. Before I left home I was given a workbook to fill out during the course of the summer. Essentially a mental preparation manual, it was filled with exercises that aided me in my visualization, goal-setting and focusing techniques as well as helping me handle the stress of the upcoming months. It had been assembled by our team psychologist, Dr. John Hogg.

I used this book to try to overcome some of the fears I had prior to the games. My first fear was that I would lose control once I arrived in the athletes' village at the end of July. In Seoul I had become intimidated by the crowds of athletes. In Barcelona I realized I had two options: I could feel inadequate and intimidated or I could feel confident and good. It came down to believing I was good enough to be there. And I knew this time I was.

My other concern was how to handle the team's performance. The schedule of events doesn't change at major games so I knew before I arrived in Barcelona that my event was to be swum on July 30th, day six of the competition, which meant I would have to sit through five days watching other events. This could work to my advantage or to my disadvantage, depending on how the team was doing. If they were doing well and achieving best performances, it would be easy for me to ride that momentum.

If they weren't doing well, I would have to somehow remove myself from their performances and create my own momentum. This would be easier said than done. If people are failing, the team starts to lose confidence. We all feed off each other's performances.

I had been through this in Seoul. It was like a

dark cloud hanging over the team. The athletes started to doubt themselves and turned to the coaches and staff for support. But they, in turn, had their own doubts. The entire group started to panic and lose confidence. I decided that if this time the team wasn't performing as well as hoped, I would remind myself of all the extra little things I had included in my preparation. By focusing on these details I hoped I would have a fresh attitude when my race day came.

Thanks to Dr. Hogg's workbook I was full of confidence because for the first time ever, before a major competition, I had a concrete plan for the upcoming months. I felt ready to go.

In organizing this summer I overlooked one thing. My plans for the Olympics ensured that things would go smoothly once I was in the village. But I hadn't thought about the long period before arriving in Barcelona. As it turned out, we were on the road for ten weeks before the Olympics. Usually when I left Canada for an extended period of time I was good at being completely focused on swimming. I got better every day I was away from home. Unfortunately this trip was different.

The first stop was Fort Lauderdale, Florida, where we trained for close to three weeks. In Florida things just weren't working for me. I am not a great fan of hot, humid weather and the entire time I was there I felt uncomfortable. I wasn't swimming well and it seemed as though I was always struggling compared to the rest of the group. I just couldn't get into the work rhythm needed to go through the heavy training periods. Every time I went to the pool I was fighting being there. I was the last at the pool and the first out. This all panicked me because I had been counting on this time to make the last big improvements I needed during this time. Instead of having a great training period I was completely losing control.

I learned in Florida that the secret to being in control doesn't just lie in being independent. It is about balance. It was great for me to have a plan but when my plan wasn't working I had to adjust. Because Deryk and I had finally learned to communicate I was able to go to him for help, and I don't think I would have made it through this period without him. I spent every second afternoon talking to him about the workouts and my own swimming, and he gave me a lot of needed reassurance and confidence. If we hadn't learned to be open before this, instead of letting myself go for advice I would have let myself sink to rock bottom before getting help, which would have been disastrous.

Now I could talk to Deryk freely. Before, if I had told him I was having trouble I would have worried that it made me look weak, but now, I realized it only made me human. Together we came up with a plan that could give me a renewed sense of control.

SUMMARY

Taking Control

Set a game plan.

Take responsibility for your actions.

Open the lines of communication.

Trust your instincts.

Sometimes before you gain control,
you have to lose it.

"I cannot do everything, but still I can do something; I will not refuse to do the something I can do."
HELEN KELLER

Mum, Dad and me at high school graduation, 1986

One of my first attempts
at public speaking, 1986

Starting at the Pan-Pacific Championships, 1987

Skin folds with Daniella Sovak, 1988

In class at the University of Calgary, 1988

Cheering on Sandy Goss at the
1988 Seoul Olympics: Tom Ponting (top),
Victor Davis (crouching) and me

Being met by RCMP officers at Calgary
on the way home from Seoul

One of my first autographs,
Calgary Airport, 1988

Post-Olympics, Calgary, 1988: from
left, Tom Ponting, Carolyn Waldo,
Prime Minister Brian Mulroney,
Michelle Cameron, me and Mila Mulroney

Waving to my family at the Summer Nationals
in Calgary, 1989

A victory jump in the pool, 1989

At the World Swimming Championships,
Perth, Australia, 1991

Canada's national team at the World
Swimming Champtionships, 1991

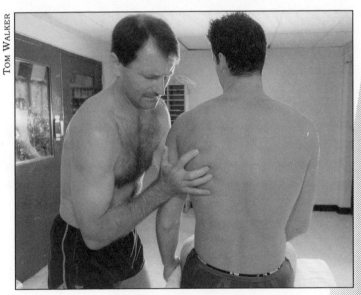

Getting a massage from
Les Wojciechowski, 1991

Jeff Rouse (first) and me (second)
at the World Championships, Perth,
1991: Jeff won by 6/100s of a second,
my lucky number a year later.

6

I May Be a Rock But I'm Not an Island

"I use not only the brain I have but
all I can borrow."
WOODROW WILSON

HEADED INTO BARCELONA FEELING VERY MUCH in control because I was part of a unified group. The power of someone who is motivated is awesome but the strength of a team is incomparable. Behind every success story there is usually a strong support group. This was certainly the case with me as I went into the Olympics.

My family, of course, was my first support group. When I started swimming it wasn't just *my* commitment, it became a lifestyle for everyone in my family. Until I was sixteen my father had to get up early in the morning to take me to the pool. When I joined the University of Calgary Swim Club it meant an extra two hours of driving time for him every day. My father's days were as long as mine—up at 5:00 A.M., work all day and then home at seven in the evening after my practice.

Most people assume that swimming isn't an expensive sport—all you need are a swimsuit and goggles. But there is a hidden cost—travel. Since there are usually a limited number of clubs in each community, we had to travel a lot to find competition. As I got better, I needed to travel further and further to compete against new athletes, and the expenses really added up. In order to help with the cost, my mother started working again. By the time I was in my teens and was seeing the world, my mother was holding down two jobs to make sure I could continue.

There were sacrifices on my part, but when one child is taking up so much of his parents' energy and income, there is sacrifice on the part of siblings as well. My brother and sister never begrudged me this, never made it an issue, even though often they would have to give up their rooms when we billeted strangers for swim meets. They got used to eating dinner at eight in the evening as opposed to six like their friends. And they never complained that I wasn't around to help out with everyday, household chores.

For the first nine years of my career my family gave me the nurturing and unconditional support that would be my base. When I moved out at seventeen, taking my hectic lifestyle with me, I felt my family could finally start to live a normal life again.

At the pool I had another support group, my team. Swimming is an individual sport, but we spent hundreds of hours with each other getting ready for competition, even though we never competed together. With my teams I developed a certain closeness, but their support was very different from that of my family. These were my co-workers, and we came together for a common goal. We formed a close bond, based not on emotions but on the sharing of physical experiences that nobody else could ever really understand. My parents could sympathize with how it felt to swim twenty kilometres, but they would never really know how that felt. Only my team-mates and I could. Of course, some team-mates became friends, even close friends, over the years, but that wasn't what I expected to find at the pool. The most important thing was that my team-mates and I supported each other through the struggles, contributing to the collective effort.

THE OUTSIDE WORLD

There came a time, when I was sixteen, that I needed a different kind of support. I wanted someone to talk with about other things.

I started spending time with my neighbour Tyrrell Clarke. Although I would get home late each evening, I could see her almost every day because she was right next door. She was older than me and was my exact opposite. I was now a "jock," in her eyes anyway, and she was an artist. We both were going through challenging periods and found a sanctuary in each other's company. I envied her seemingly carefree life and she envied my single-minded pursuit. Of course, I never stopped to think of the real picture. She was unemployed, living at home and working in a studio in her parents' basement. And she never thought about the hours I spent going back and forth in the pool.

With Tyrrell I started to do some of those spontaneous, impulsive things I had wanted to do when I was younger. I would sneak out late at night with her to cafés and restaurants. We would talk and laugh for hours.

My favourite time was spent on her parents' porch in the evening. We would sit and watch the sun go down and see the stars come out. I would talk about my dreams and so would Tyrrell, neither of us having any preconceived ideas of what the other could or couldn't do. When things were driving me crazy, which was often in my late teens, and I would feel like running away from everything, I would plot a trip with Tyrrell. We would dream of leaving it all behind and going off to Europe. It would never pan out, of course, but it was a good escape. What I was getting from Tyrrell was emotional support.

HELP

These three groups—my family, team-mates and friends—remained a crucial part of my success. They each provided me with different kinds of support but they were equally important.

There have been a couple of times in my life when I would have taken an entirely different path had it not been for help from my support systems. One of those periods was after the 1988 Olympics. I became good at asking various people their opinions on subjects before I made up my mind. I would try to weigh all the different outlooks and take the best ideas from each person to mould a solution for myself. My support groups became my sounding board.

After 1988 I came very close to retiring from swimming. I had been to the games and won a medal, and my mission was accomplished in one sense. I was ready to head into new areas. When I returned from the Olympics I had thought that I would become a celebrity overnight and make quite a living for myself. Dream on. I did get an increase in government support, though, from $550 a month to $650. But life was not exactly what I had imagined.

I will never forget the disappointment of arriving home from Seoul. I was on the same plane as Michelle Cameron, who had won a gold medal in synchronized swimming. When we pulled up to the terminal in Calgary the plane was greeted by an RCMP escort. For Michelle. She was being escorted up to a greeting party and she kept turning around and looking for me, asking the RCMP to slow down so I could join them. I realized at that moment that my dreams of celebrity weren't going to materialize. Nobody knew who this silver medallist from the relay was.

To make matters worse, I didn't know if the public was going to cheer me or interrogate me, as I was a part of the Olympic team that had disappointed many Canadians because of the steroid scandal. It was not the best of times to be a Canadian Olympian.

Before I made any rash decisions about my future, I took some time completely away from my sport. I didn't retire but I didn't go back right away either. I wanted to weigh all the options.

During this time I had three conversations that had an enormous impact on my decision. The first was with my father. I asked him how he would feel if I retired. He told me he was really proud of everything that had happened to me in my career, and whatever I chose to do would be fine with him. If I still swam, it would be a bonus, as far as he was concerned. These words were exactly what I needed to hear. I knew that whatever I chose to do would be accepted by my parents.

My second conversation was with a great friend of mine, Hilda Brownlee, the athletic service director from Swimming Canada. I met Hilda when I was fourteen and we hit it off right away. I asked her what she thought of the idea of my retirement. She was really honest with me and told me what I didn't want to hear. She knew I was disappointed from my summer's results and said that if I retired I would spend the rest of my life wondering "What if..." I reminded her that I had a silver medal—all I had ever really wanted. But she called my bluff and told me she knew I had always wanted to win an individual medal at the Olympics. She was right.

After talking to Hilda and my father, I was really torn over what to do. I decided to turn to someone who had been through this before. One of my idols from the 1976 Olympics had been Diane Jones. Like me, she had had a disappointing experience. After 1976 she had to decide if it was worth committing herself to four more years of work. Diane chose to continue and train, only to find her work would go unrewarded because Canada boycotted the Moscow Games. If anyone could share my feelings, it would be Diane.

In 1988 she was working in Calgary with the Alberta Sport Council and I arranged for an appointment to talk to her. Instead of giving me any advice, Diane listened to everything I had to say, then made a suggestion. She was providing a training program, through the Alberta Sport Council, for athletes to learn to give public speeches, and she thought it would be a good idea if I took the course before I made any decisions. I agreed.

For sixteen hours, I took an incredibly condensed two-day program. I learned the basics of what to do in front of an audience but I was extremely rough. I couldn't help but do everything you weren't supposed to do, but I really liked the challenge of getting up in front of an audience. When the course was over, on a Sunday, I decided to put this training to use at once. I phoned up Diane on Monday morning and asked her to get me into the schools to share my Olympic story. She made the contacts for me and a week later I started visiting grade schools in Calgary.

Over the next couple of months I spoke at more than twenty-five schools. I loved it. My stories were so well received by my audiences that I started to feel good about being an Olympian again. By the end of the fall I had literally talked myself back into swimming. In showing people the positive side of the games I also reminded myself.

FINANCIAL SUPPORT

In January 1989 I went back to the pool. Starting back was difficult because it wasn't just a time commitment, it was a career decision. If I wanted to be the best in the world it would be impossible to go to school or work full time for the next four years. Even though I wanted to go back to university, I put that on hold. As a swimmer I was making six hundred and fifty dollars a month. This wasn't even close to the amount of money I would need to compete seriously internationally. I knew that if I were to have any chance in the next four years I would have to find ways to supplement my income.

Some of my team-mates had part-time jobs waiting tables or landscaping to help make ends meet. As a result they missed a lot of training. I knew this wasn't an option for me because I couldn't afford to miss any training time. I had won an Olympic medal and figured that must be worth something, so I started looking for potential sponsors.

As I was knocking on doors, trying to get sponsorship, I found that nothing comes from nothing. I would have to offer something in return for financial support, but bathing suits don't leave much room for corporate logos. This is when I began to put my public-speaking training to use.

I was a client of the Investors Group, putting away a very small amount of money every month. My representative at this time, Ray Simundson, asked me if I would like to give a speech at his office. I accepted, thinking this might lead to sponsorship.

This was my first speech to a business group, and I was paralysed with fear. I was far more nervous than I was before swimming in the Olympic final. I didn't know if my message would be appropriate. I thought my presentation to the schools was too basic to give to a business group so I tried to make it more sophisticated. I made some of the anecdotes more business oriented, but never actually being in business myself, I didn't know if I was on the right track.

Halfway through my speech I got confused about which anecdote to use next and went blank, so I reverted to the only material I knew, my grade-school presentation. The audience was pretty quiet and I couldn't figure out if they were quiet because I was so good or if they were just bored. I kept going, praying for the end. After twenty minutes I was finished and I received a nice round of applause, but I knew I hadn't been very good. I certainly wasn't polished, but I had enthusiasm. And I won their support.

The company's regional manager, George Thomson, believed in me and sponsored me. In return, I spoke to many different Investors groups, and the more I did, the better I became. This local sponsorship led eventually to a contract with the head office in Winnipeg. For three years I travelled the country speaking to their representatives during my off-time from swimming.

As I prepared for the Olympics, I was financially sound for the next couple of years. And I also had thousands of people from coast to coast on my support team.

SYNERGY

One year away from the Olympics I knew I had to work harder and do more than I had ever done before in my life to make my dreams come true. I also understood I couldn't do it alone. Each one of my support groups would play a major role in helping me get through the process.

The first part was always there for me, of course. My family knew I wouldn't be in Calgary much that year but accepted my absence. I would be away for every major holiday, including Christmas.

My swimming group was very small, only fourteen of us, but strong. Over the past twelve months we had travelled the world together, and as we went along, we became very much like an extended family, each of us taking on certain roles to make training more bearable.

We were led by our coach, Deryk, who had the unenviable task of keeping us all in line and on track. Then there was the old man on the team, Tom Ponting. Tom had been in two Olympics already and was by far the most experienced among us at twenty-seven years of age. He was the cynic, with a wicked sense of humour. On the other side of the scale was Curtis Myden, our hope for the future. He was being touted as the next Alex Baumann, no easy shoes to fill. Curtis was only seventeen, the youngest of the group. In between, there were the jokers, Darren Ward, Andrea Nugent and myself. We were the goofballs who always did stupid things to help create a light atmosphere and to keep people laughing. We worked hard when we had to but always found some way to have fun. There were the amazing workout swimmers, Robby McFarlane, Gary Vandermeulen, Sean Swain and Erin Holland. Though they only had an outside chance of making the Olympic team, they formed the backbone of the group. When training got tough these guys would pull the group through. There were the sprinters,

Jessica Amey, Steven Vandermeulen and Kathy Monar. They were the ones who set the pace in the sprints for all of us to follow. Finally there was Jon Cleveland. He was one of the most talented swimmers and also one of the most intense. He did every single workout like there was no tomorrow.

When we were all thrown together we formed an incredibly strong unit. But this closeness took many years to form.

UNLIKELY PARTNERS

In 1986 I travelled with six members of my swim club to Russia. The Russians had invited us to train with some of their top athletes in the city of Sukumi, on the Black Sea across from Turkey. It was a resort area for the Communist Party so even though we were going to the Soviet Union, we had high hopes. A resort was a resort, after all.

There was one catch. We were allowed to train with the Russians but only if we completely integrated with them. Our Canadian coaches weren't permitted to help with the training program. We were in the hands of a foreign coach. This was the first time for such an experience, because Deryk usually played a big role, even if we were training with another club.

On the first day, I remember meeting the swimmers I would be spending the next couple of weeks with. I was lucky, because I had two team-mates in my group, Andrea Nugent and Tom Ponting, to help soften the blow of meeting the Russians. When we were introduced to them they looked at us with stone cold faces. One guy in particular, Sergei Zobolotnov, made a huge fuss. He yelled at his coach and stomped off, complaining about having to train with me. Sergei was ranked number two in the world in the backstroke and he didn't want to help some upstart kid from Canada who was fourth. We were not off to a good start. Andrea, Tom and I looked at each other and shrugged. I was afraid it was going to be a long two weeks.

None of the Russian swimmers or coaches in our group spoke any English, so everything we had to do was communicated through hand signals. There were many times when I didn't know what I was supposed to be doing, so I would just do whatever I could to fit in. I ended up getting yelled at in Russian a lot. Andrea and Tom would either be yelled at as well or would be laughing at me. It was quite an adventure.

The kind of work we did was outrageous. The Soviet equipment was from the 1960s, outdated and very basic. Somehow the Russians did things with those machines that I had never thought of. Twice every day we would spend one hour in the gym before swimming for two hours. We would climb and jump and throw and push more than I ever imagined humanly possible. It was so strenuous that most mornings I would wake up so stiff and sore that I could barely move. One thought would run through my mind: I would have to do it all over again today. It was torturous. The only thing that kept me going was the support I received from my teammates. When I wanted to give up, Tom and Andrea wouldn't let me. We had built a strong bond, and together we made it through this training.

The incredible thing was that over the course of the two weeks the Soviet swimmers also started to bond with us. They weren't superhuman and the training was hard for them, too. At the end of the training camp we still couldn't speak a word to each other, but we had shared the same pain and survived. Through it we had moved from being opposing teams to supporting each other. We shared a feeling known only to those of us going through this experience. That powerful thought brings you very close to people, even if they are virtual strangers.

In the Barcelona Olympic year when our team

travelled to Australia, it was very much the same thing. Before we would do those crazy heart-rate sets at five in the morning we would gather in a small room. It would be very quiet. We were all scared of the pain we were about to go through but by sitting together for a few minutes quietly we drew strength from each other. The travelling as a team around the world, the training in Russia, watching each other go through tough periods gave us great empathy for each other. We didn't need to speak about every part of training, we understood what the others were feeling and going through.

OUTSIDE HELP

My team-mates couldn't be with me twenty-four hours a day, and I didn't want them to be. This is when my third support group became a factor. When I left the pool, it was really important for me to escape the team for a while. Sometimes I needed to be around people who had no preconceived ideas about my potential so I could share my dreams. I needed help from people outside my immediate swimming group.

For years our team had worked with a physiologist, Dr. Dave Smith. He became more than just an adviser to me on swimming matters, he became a very close friend. When I was feeling really frustrated or doubtful I would talk to Doc and invariably feel better. He would first make me feel confident about what I was doing physically, as far as training was concerned. Then he would make me feel good about being me. I could yell at him and complain to him and he understood the roots of my frustration. I would always leave his office feeling as though the weight of the world had been lifted off my shoulders.

Doc had a team of people working with him that were also a great help. Most of them were graduate students who knew nothing about swimming before they started working with us. I could talk to them about normal, everyday things—movies, music, politics, travel. They provided a valuable balance to my life.

Diane Jones, now Diane Jones Konihowski, was again an important part of my year. She was someone I went to often when the pressure of preparing for the games began getting to me. In the months leading up to the games, medal hopefuls are scrutinized and are approached by the media for interviews and profiles. This can be flattering, but also draining on the training schedule. It was with Diane's help that I decided that after a certain day I would give no more interviews, and would focus only on my swimming.

As far as swimming was concerned, there was one area where my team-mates and my coach couldn't help me. One part of my race that needed some serious attention was the last fifteen metres. I always died during this portion of the swim, because I didn't have the muscle power to finish the race with the same physical strength with which I started. I knew that the weight program I was following was good, but it wasn't specific enough for my needs. Something had to change.

Fortunately our team worked with a weight coach I really trusted, Geoff Gregson. He came up with a plan for my Olympic year. Instead of just doing heavy weight training he wanted me to focus on exercises that were specific to the backstroke. This was very hard to do using normal weight machines so we decided to try something else. Once I had built up my power using the conventional methods, we switched to a medicine ball which is a ball bound in leather and filled with sand, weighing anywhere from five pounds upward. By throwing it different ways you can get a great strength workout. The only drawback is you need somebody equally strong to catch it and throw it to you. Because the exercises I was doing were so specific to the backstroke, none of my team-mates, who swam other strokes, could work with me on this.

Every Tuesday and Thursday Geoff would come to the weight room and spend an hour throwing the medicine ball back and forth with me. He gave up his lunch hours to help me get stronger. Without his support I would never have received the weight training I needed.

UTILIZING THE STRENGTHS OF PEOPLE AROUND YOU

In my day-to-day training I came into contact with two people whose job it was to look after my physical well-being. By spending many hours with them I learned they had great advice to offer as well as their skills. It is surprising sometimes what a hidden wealth of knowledge is around you.

During bouts of really heavy training we would receive massage. For more than six years I worked with the same masseur, Les Wojciechowski, who was extremely well trained and capable. Going to see Les meant more than just getting a massage. For me it was like hav-ing a thirty-minute dose of positive reinforce-ment. Les would tell me the positive effects training was having on my body, and he could tell what kind of shape I was in just by feeling my muscles. His words sometimes meant more to me than his massage. Usually when I went to see him I was in a very heavy training period and would be overtired and overtrained. By spending time with him, my self-confidence was boosted when I really needed it. After seeing him I was always ready for the next practice, mentally and physically.

Every couple of weeks our group would have to go see Daniella Sovak for skin-fold testing to measure our body fat and muscle growth. For fifteen minutes she would pinch different parts of my body with callipers, from my cheek down to my ankles, to see how much body fat I had. Once she was done with the callipers she would measure the circumference of my arms, legs, etc., to see how my muscles were holding up. This was a key part of the training program, because if my fat levels went too low it meant I would be close to breaking down. If my muscle bulk got too high, it could be detrimental to swimming fast. It really was a science.

I had been doing this testing since I was sixteen years old, and over the course of those years the fifteen-minute sessions with Daniella added up to a significant number of hours. We became good friends and I held a deep admiration for her. She had been a champion figure skater as a youth in Czechoslovakia and had defected to the West in her twenties. When she left, she was aware that serious penalties might be imposed on her family, and one member of her family who needed medical treatment might not receive care. But she decided to leave, hoping she would be able to send help back to her family. She had to make the decision, no one else could make it for her. In the end, everything worked out, and now she can even go back home to visit.

When I was going through tough times, Daniella would remind me of her story. When I questioned what I was doing she would give me this advice: "You can listen to everyone else's point of view but in the end you have to make the decision for yourself. Do what you think is right. Trust yourself." She was much more to me than just a person who measured skin-folds. She was the one person who always reminded me it was ultimately my decision to make my own choices in life.

HOME SWEET HOME

The closer we came to the Olympics, the more we were on the road as a team. It was great for training but sometimes it was hard on me emotionally. I missed the support group I had built at home. And if I was on the road too much, I would feel that I didn't belong anywhere.

In April my swimming team travelled to Hawaii for their last bout of training before the Olympic trials, but I didn't join them. I decided that I needed this last stretch of time to just be at home and feel familiar with my surroundings. That was more important to me than training. It was a tough decision because I would miss swimming with my group, but I knew I needed this time at home to recharge.

I surrounded myself with my friends. I would hang out at home with my room-mate, Lisa. We would have friends over and do anything but talk about sports. I swam with our club's assistant coach, Mike Blondal, and really enjoyed the change of coaching style for a couple of weeks. I would go to movies, see old friends, have dinner at my parents', take some time for myself. I became re-energized. I had been at the point where the thought of getting on another plane made me feel sick. This stretch at home was long overdue.

This period gave me a chance to see everybody I wanted to see, and helped me appreciate the support that was building for my effort that summer. When I walked around the city, many people came up and wished me well, making me feel very proud. At times during my Olympic preparation I had felt isolated but in the last stages I didn't feel that way at all. On May 24th, when I hopped on the plane for the final training phase and was leaving Canada, I felt as though I had an incredible force behind me. The support at home left me empowered.

SUMMARY

Teamwork

Surround yourself with
positive people.

Listen to others but follow
your instincts.

Be supportive.

Success for one team member
breeds success for all.

The sum of the whole is greater
than the parts.

"No matter what accomplishments you
make, somebody helps you."
WILMA RUDOLF

7

Metamorphosis

"Only those who are afraid to fear,
fear too much. Strength is not the
absence of weakness but how we
wrestle with our weaknesses."
NOAH BENSHEA

"ONE IS THE LONELIEST NUMBER" WENT A LINE from a song that was popular when I was growing up. Little did I know how true these lyrics were, though I was soon to find out. When I was coming up through the ranks, Victor Davis and Alex Baumann and Gaetan Boucher and Carolyn Waldo were all Olympic champions. My dream was to be one too someday, but I never really completely believed that it was possible. I could not imagine myself winning and being in their company. They were what champions were made of. Surely I wasn't cut from the same cloth.

I think many of us feel this way, regardless of what we do. It is great to watch other people succeed but it is hard to see that success for ourselves. It is so much easier to settle for something less. This is certainly how I felt.

The thought of being the best in the world was a nice one but it seemed to me I could be content being one of the better competitors. Who needs all the pressure that goes along with being the best? I always fell back on the thought, "As long as I am my best I will be happy." The problem was, what was my best?

There was a time in my career when I was literally a fingernail away from being the very best but I still couldn't see myself on top. I was content to just keep plugging along, never thinking I could actually be the best. In fact, when I was second, I worried that someone was going to come up from behind and knock me off that position anyway. I didn't yet consider winning as a viable option for myself. I was willing to settle for something less.

There was one particular moment in my life when I had to make a choice. I could keep being a second- or fourth- or tenth-place swimmer or I could be the best. I had the opportunity to make a breakthrough. The decision was mine, but it was incredibly hard to make. If I chose to, I would be breaking the cycle and things would never be the same again.

WHY NOT ME?

I was confronted with this in 1990. I had just travelled through Europe competing in the World Cup circuit. It had been a terrific trip for me and I really considered the season over once I had completed my last World Cup race. Unfortunately I still had one competition left. Upon returning to Canada I would have to swim in the Canadian nationals.

The nationals in the winter of 1990 were held in Saskatoon. No offence to beautiful Saskatoon but I had just travelled through Europe for three weeks and this was about the last place I wanted to be. There wasn't a choice, though. I had to swim to support my team. Reluctantly I headed to the meet, but I really wasn't concentrating on swimming. I was just showing up because I felt an obligation.

On the second day of the competition I swam the 100-metre backstroke. In the morning heats I didn't get too ready because qualifying for the final was more of a technicality than anything. I swam in the last heat of the event. I sat and watched the other swimmers race until it was finally my turn. The times weren't too fast from the previous heats so I could take it relatively easy in my swim.

I dove in and felt surprisingly great. I was really relaxed and wasn't pushing myself too hard. When I finished the swim I looked up at the scoreboard and couldn't believe my eyes. I had swum 54.56, less than four-tenths off the world record.

I realized immediately that in the evening I would have another shot at this world record. So did everybody else in the building. As I was leaving the pool I had all sorts of people giving me knowing looks. They thought I was going to do something great that evening.

The break between the heats and finals was

like nothing I had ever been through before. I lay down and tried to rest but every time I closed my eyes my heart-rate would quadruple. For the first time in my life I had a chance to be the very best in the world at something and I was scared. I spent hours picturing myself winning and doing the victory jump as I had seen Graham Smith and Alex Baumann do when I was growing up. Somehow this just didn't seem right with me in the picture. Half of me wanted to do it and the other half was thinking about all the pressure that goes with being the best in the world. I was torn between thinking I could do it and being absolutely horrified at the thought of it.

I really had two options. I could just miss the record and still have a great swim or I could let myself go and try to be the very best. I was afraid to try to break the record and fail. I was also afraid of the thought of doing something nobody had ever done before.

I went back to the pool to get ready for the final. I still hadn't come to terms with what I was going to do but I went through the warm-up, preparing as best I could. There was a strange air around the pool that evening. Everyone was quiet whenever I walked by. Coaches and swimmers would watch me with a confident look in their eyes. It was a bit unnerving. They made me feel very supported but also apprehensive. What if I let everybody down?

As the race approached I became more and more excited. The air in the pool was heavily chlorinated and I was having a tough time breathing. I decided to escape it for a few minutes before the race, and I walked outside where it was cold but crisp and fresh. It gave me a little jolt. I remember thinking about a lot of things. As my mind was churning I looked across the way and saw the Saskatoon skyline. There was the small city in the distance with the mill in the forefront. Looking at this scene gave me a sense of calm. Up until this moment I had thought about swimming 54.21. The world record for the 100-metre backstroke was 54.20. It would be a great swim but I would just miss the world record. I wouldn't have to deal with the pressure of being the best.

This made me feel safe as I thought of it over and over. But when I looked at the peace of the city something hit me. I realized that whether I broke the record or not, nothing was going to really change. It would be something great for me, but in the grand scheme of things the world would go on. By the same token, there would be no harm done if I missed it.

A new thought entered my mind. Why not me? Somebody had to be the best. Surely I was as good a candidate as anybody else. I took a couple of breaths of fresh air and realized I had to give this everything I had. Right now I was being given a chance to be the best, a chance that doesn't come around too often. I decided I wasn't going to let my fears hold me back any more. I would let myself go and see if I had what it takes to be the very best.

I went back into the pool and did my final preparation for the race. I said to myself over and over, let yourself go, swim fast and easily, enjoy this opportunity. I could hear the pool fall silent as they announced the finalists for the 100-metre backstroke. There was a great sense of anticipation. I was introduced and there was an enormous cheer. I looked down the pool and saw that people were everywhere. Nobody was even warming up for the next races. They were all watching. I felt ready to go.

During the race I could tell I was swimming fast. The roar was so loud I could hear it even in the water. The race is four lengths long, and on the last length I was so tired I could barely move. I could hear the crowd louder than ever, though, and figured I had to be close if they were cheering this loudly. Time seemed to be in slow motion. I remember hitting the wall and turning to look at the scoreboard. I couldn't believe what I saw: 53.69. I had broken the old short-course world record by over half a second. The swimmers and spectators were going wild. I did a double-take and then did what I had dreamed of that afternoon: I did my victory jump as I had seen my idols do. And unlike my dream earlier in the day, it felt just right.

I really don't know what I was afraid of before. This was one of the greatest moments of my life. It felt so incredibly good to be the best, to be my best. I felt so satisfied that I had faced my fears. Maybe that is what made this moment that much better. I had been so afraid and had had such preconceived ideas of what it would feel like. And I had been so wrong. This felt peaceful instead of frightening. I would have never known this had I not been able to overcome my own fears.

I learned on this day about the magic of life. You can try something a thousand times and never get it just right, but sometimes if you do it just one more time you get a magical moment. This is what happened to me. I had swum this race so many times in my life, but on this one day my mind and body were totally in sync. I had gone from being a good swimmer to being the best in the world. A metamorphosis had taken place. I would never be quite the same again.

SUMMARY

Overcoming Weaknesses

Fears and doubts will paralyse you.

Look at your options and
make a choice.

Don't be frightened by change.

"Destiny is not a matter of chance,
it is a matter of choice..."
WILLIAM JENNINGS BRYAN

8

Did I Ever
Tell You
You're My Hero?

"All of that excellence belongs to me.
I will use it, take it all into myself
and delight in it. Then I become
more excellent myself."
MAYA ANGELOU

O NE OF THE MOST ENJOYABLE THINGS IN LIFE IS spending time with people, hearing them tell of their experiences. By listening well, you can make another's experience like your own. It is impossible for me to tell my own story without mentioning some of the people who have had an influence on me. From the time I was eight years old and watched the 1976 Olympics on TV until the day before my own Olympic performance, other people helped me remain motivated. By sharing in their excellence I was inspired to reach for my own.

I was very lucky that this was something I learned early on at school. In grade six I had a teacher, Mrs. McCowan, who was very open and down to earth. She seemed to know where we were coming from and as her students we had an easy time relating to her. In Mrs. McCowan's class it was okay to talk about things, to think out loud. She encouraged us to challenge each other and her with questions about anything.

This was really important because the school I attended had a wide variety of students. We were mainly from middle-income families, but there were kids from broken and abusive homes, visible minorities and children of lower-income families as well. Somehow we had to learn to live together.

With Mrs. McCowan's help we figured out how. In a very subtle way, she knew how to teach us to appreciate each other's achievements. Whenever somebody did something that was kind of special she would announce it to the class. The achievement didn't have to be in a school activity. For example, if someone had scored in a hockey game or played the piano well, Mrs. McCowan would recognize them. She did it in such a way that by the end of the first few months of school everybody had been mentioned at least once. Every single person in the class was recognized, not just a few stand-outs. By trying to make each of us feel proud of our achievements, and allowing us to share them with our peers, she was able to create an atmosphere of tolerance among us. It not only helped us appreciate others but it encouraged each of us to try to excel to be recognized ourselves.

Although this may sound somewhat saccharine and sweet, it's true. There is greatness around us, it's just a matter of looking for it. If you are cynical about excellence you will never recognize it, in others or yourself.

It was largely because of this example that at an early age I learned to look past envy and spite and to recognize the good around me. I experienced first-hand how good it felt to share in someone else's accomplishments. In effect we became role models for each other.

This lesson was easily transferred to my swimming. It wasn't hard to find great accomplishments—even on a small scale—if you just looked for them. I was usually the youngest swimmer in my group, so my role models tended to be older.

USING OTHERS' EXCELLENCE

By 1984 I was swimming in the top group at the University of Calgary Swim Club. Many of my team-mates were training with one specific goal in mind: to compete in the Summer Olympics to be held in Los Angeles that year. I was sixteen years old, and although I would have loved to swim in L.A., realistically I was too young. My event was filled with Canadians who were top world-ranked swimmers and the chance of my qualifying was very slim. It would just be great to go to the Olympic trials and gain some experience.

Before every major games there is a trial meet where the best Canadians compete for spots on the team. Because the Olympics have become such an enormous spectacle, each country is allowed to send only its top two swimmers in each event. In many cases there are at least four people within striking distance of each other, all competing for the same two spots. The trials are often filled with drama and disappointment. Inevitably there are surprises, someone comes from nowhere and makes the team. There are also many close races where one of the world's best swimmers just can't put it all together on the day. If you are not one of the top two at the trials, you don't go on to the Olympics.

In June I travelled with my team to Toronto to compete in my first Olympic trials. Throughout the year I had been surrounded by these swimmers who were striving to be the best. They had become my role models. According to conventional wisdom, I wasn't supposed to make the Olympic team, but somewhere along the way I forgot. The idea of going to the Olympics was taken for granted by the people around me and I got caught up in this way of thinking. By the time we actually went to the trials I considered myself a contender.

The meet was held at the Etobicoke Olympium. The place only holds a couple of hundred spectators, but it was packed with friends and families cheering on their own. Needless to say, the mood in the building was tense. As each race finished, the story was always the same: there were two swimmers who were ecstatic and at least a couple of others who were stunned at the results. I didn't swim until the end of the program, so I watched from the stands most of the time.

I was riding an emotional roller-coaster, feeling great for the people who made it onto the team but miserable for some of the third- and fourth-place finishers. I had to wait three days before my own swim. I wasn't used to this kind of waiting period and it was agonizing. But in some ways it was also inspiring, watching as some people rose to the challenge.

One race really stood out in my mind. It was the women's 400 individual medley. The winner was a woman named Donna McGinnis, from Edmonton. The drama came in the race for second place between two others, Kathy Richardson and Natalie Gingras. They were both respected swimmers but the sentimental favourite was Kathy. She had been named to the 1980 Olympic team but didn't get to compete because of the boycott. She decided to continue swimming so she could have a chance at competing in the 1984 Olympics. This race was her only real opportunity at making the team.

The individual medley is a race where all four strokes are swum. Because each swimmer has his or her own specialties the positioning of the athletes changes a lot in the course of the race. It is very exciting to watch. The race between Natalie and Kathy went back and forth for the entire four hundred metres. Where Natalie was weak Kathy was strong and vice versa. Finally it came down to the last hundred metres of the race, which is freestyle. Kathy was ahead going into it but Natalie was known for her strength in this last part. Kathy was fighting with everything she had but she just couldn't hold back Natalie's charge. The race was so close I had to look at the scoreboard to find out who had won the position on the Olympic team. By a few tenths of a second Natalie had won the battle. She would be going to the Olympics. Kathy, who had spent four years training for this moment, would have to live with third.

I will never forget the contrast between the two swimmers in the water. Natalie's entire team rushed over to be with her and there was a great celebration at the end of her lane. On the other side of the pool, Kathy was alone holding her face in her hands. She wasn't a poor sport, but her disappointment was so acute she couldn't hide it. I empathized with both of them: I could relate to Natalie's pure joy but I also appreciated the effort Kathy had given and the despair she was feeling, realizing that after four years of work her dream had been wiped out in a few seconds. That image of losing stayed with me for a long time but it also awakened in me a compassion for those who would suffer as a consequence of my success. I realized that sharing in another's excellence had to include the moments of defeat as well as those of triumph. Life challenges us to deal with both success and failure.

A few days later it was my turn to swim. As much as I would have loved to make the team, my competition was too strong. I ended up fifth in the final. I remembered Kathy and reminded myself that, unlike her, I still had many chances ahead of me.

As I had so many years earlier, I found myself glued to the television watching the Olympics. I had always been a fan but this time the games held a new meaning for me because I had been a part of the process, even though I hadn't made it. I had seen the team being selected. I was especially interested in watching the backstroke events. Maybe it was crazy but I thought that I had had something to do with these guys competing. Because they had beaten me, I felt I had helped them get there in some way.

When two Canadians, Cam Henning and Mike West, won bronze medals in the backstroke I was ecstatic. One thing I hadn't realized until then was that Canada's high standard in the backstroke event forced me to be that much better myself just to make a team. I also understood that because of our country's high world rankings my chances for an eventual Olympic medal were very good.

MOTIVATION THROUGH INSPIRATION

Many times I have been asked what kept me motivated. There were different sources of inspiration but perhaps the most important was that the excellence I saw in all forms around me made me realize my own potential. Though my heroes were often athletes, they didn't have to be.

At times throughout my career my own motivation was really low. I was working so hard that my spirit was sometimes dampened by the sheer physical labour of training. At these times I searched for some form of excellence in someone else to keep me going. Greatness is always out there. Something as simple as the lyrics in a song, an inspiring book, a show on TV, or a motivating movie can rekindle your spirit. It doesn't matter what the medium is that inspires you, as long as you are open to being inspired.

February of 1992 was one of the hardest months in my Olympic preparation. When the Winter Olympics opened, I realized how little time I had before it was my turn. I had real doubts about whether I was on track. My self-confidence fluctuated wildly. One day I would have a great workout and feel everything was fine, and then the next day something would be a little off and I would panic. This all came to a head on February 11th. I had a little break-down; I couldn't get in the pool for the workout. As Deryk was having the team meeting before practice and reading out the sets, I was feeling the bile rise in my throat. When the meeting ended and my team-mates were getting in the water, I looked at Deryk and that was all it took. Deryk and I decided the best thing would be for me to take a few days off and relax. His advice to me was to do anything I wanted, to make sure that I recharged myself because there was still a long way to go.

I decided to just stay around the house and try to get grounded. On February 15th I felt I had been a hermit long enough so I planned to go and meet some friends for coffee in the morn-ing. It was a Saturday. As I was getting ready to go out I flicked on the TV. I didn't sit and watch but as I was running around I kept hearing Kerrin-Lee Gartner's name being announced. This was the day of the women's downhill at the Winter Olympics. I finally sat and watched and saw that Kerrin's time was in the corner of the screen, meaning she had the fastest run of the morning so far. There were skiers still to finish the course but Kerrin was the leader at this point. Nobody beat the time that was on the screen. Kerrin-Lee Gartner had won the Olympic downhill.

Something hit me really hard that day. Maybe it was because Kerrin was from Calgary and she had never won a big race before so no one expected her to win this one, or maybe it was because I was so desperate to boost my own confidence. Whatever the case, I couldn't move for the next couple of hours. I just sat there watching the highlights over and over. Finally the medal presentation was shown. Kerrin jumped up onto the top podium and was so excited she couldn't stand still. I saw the Canadian flag being raised and heard our anthem being played, and I felt moved for Kerrin. Then I watched her being interviewed with her husband, Max, in the studio. Their joy and shock were absolutely clear.

I realized that in a few months I would have my chance at a moment just like this one. I recognized the similarities between the two of us, both underdogs from Calgary. Most importantly, I recognized that I had the potential to win. By sharing in Kerrin's day I found the spark I needed to carry on my own journey for the next little while.

THE LITTLE THINGS

We are all surrounded by excellence, and all too often we take it for granted. Sometimes I would take a step back and look at everything those around us were doing to help us. The effort and commitment that volunteers and parents gave so freely and unconditionally to provide us with opportunities was another form of excellence. The little things like officiating at our swim meets and working at fund-raisers were vital to the effort. They knew there was no guarantee any of us would succeed, they just wanted to make sure we had every opportunity in our attempt. Their work on our behalf was inspirational.

Once in a while I would stumble upon excellence in the most unlikely places. In the summer of 1992 I came back from workout one day and flicked on the television. The channel was on the "Oprah Winfrey Show" and her topic was excellence. It may sound ludicrous to say that I found inspiration from a TV talk show, but I did. For the next hour I sat and listened to five different success stories. The person who had the

most influence on me was an incredibly elo-
quent woman, poet Maya Angelou. She inspired
me. Her main message was that we should all
take delight in the excellence of others. Take it
all in, surround yourself with it, then turn it
around and make it your own. Don't separate
yourself from excellence, share in it.

I really heard Maya Angelou. Throughout the
rest of my Olympic preparation I thought of her
words often. This is your life, she said. *This is
your life.* I wanted my life to be the best it could
be.

YOU DON'T HAVE TO WIN TO BE EXCELLENT
In May 1992 I travelled with the University of
Calgary Swim Club to the Olympic trials in
Montreal. I had been pre-selected to the
Olympic team because my time was ranked
among the top three in the world, so I would not
have to be in top form at this competition. I was
the only Canadian in this position. The rest of
my peers would have to go through the sudden-
death situation of being in the top two on the
day.

As always, there were some big surprises at
the meet. I watched as the days passed and
some very close friends and team-mates didn't
qualify for the team. I found it hard to face two

people in particular, Keltie Duggan, a breast-stroker, and Sandy Goss, a freestyler. They were both long-time national team members and if they had been in top form they would have had no problem making the team. Unfortunately on this day things just weren't right. Neither one of them qualified to represent Canada that summer in Barcelona.

I knew I should talk to them, but it was very difficult. What do you say to a friend at a moment like this? I wasn't really too sure, but I just knew I had to say something.

When I saw Keltie I could tell she was having a hard time. I think a lot of people had been coming up to her and telling her how sorry they felt for her, which was just making things worse. She was reliving her race over and over again. I wanted to say something that would make her feel better. When I talked to Keltie I thought back to some of the great moments she had had on some of the national team trips. She had been Commonwealth and Pan American champion in her career. She had represented Canada at the 1988 Olympics. There was a lot of good there. This is what we talked about instead of her race today. Towards the end of our conversation she was smiling, but I could still see the sadness in her eyes. She was still focusing on her performance on this day. Again I reminded her of something. "One swim does not make a career. Look at the entire package. You have done some really great things as an athlete. Today you had a good swim that came up short but that doesn't make you any less of a champion. You can look back on your career and feel very proud. It's filled with excellence." She gave me the biggest hug. And I hope she realized that whatever the outcome, the real accomplishment lies in the journey not in the arrival.

I believe very strongly in what I told Keltie. In our world, performances are often judged by what people see on one particular day. This is not what constitutes a career. It is the striving and reaching in the day-to-day struggle that takes place year after year that we must remember in times of trouble or defeat.

This thought really helped in my own approach to the Olympics. I tried not to think of winning or losing that one swim. I began to think of it as one more experience in a growing portfolio, albeit a very important one.

RECOGNIZING THE COMPETITION

It's one thing to delight in the excellence of your team-mates and friends. It's another thing entirely to take delight in watching your competition.

This was one thing I had never been good at, but it was something I needed to tackle before the Olympics.

Maya Angelou had touched on this. She had said she refused to separate herself from *any* form of excellence. She would set no boundaries but instead would marvel at it in *all* of its many forms to become better herself. White, black, Asian, gay, straight, woman, man—she would not discriminate. I remembered this the day we travelled to the dual meet against the Americans two weeks before the Olympics. In spite of all the plans I had and all the positive thoughts I was thinking, I was still obsessed with the performance of my competitors. I couldn't share in their excellence, I still felt too threatened by it.

The minute we arrived at the meet I thought to myself: Okay, I'm not going to look for the guys I'm racing against; I'm going to avoid them at all costs. And, of course, the first thing I did was look everywhere for them. I couldn't help myself.

When I found them they looked pretty good but not any different than I had remembered— two arms, two legs, etc. But when they went into the water it was like magic. All through the warm-up I kept looking underwater to see their starts and turns. It was like nothing I had ever seen. I had been working on my underwater kick now for a long time but it wasn't even close to being as good as these guys'. They looked like dolphins. I watched and watched until finally warm-up was over.

In the dual meet I had the opportunity to see their starts again. When Jeff Rouse did his, the Canadian team members actually held their breath and turned to look at me. A bunch of the guys asked me, "Did you see that?" "Yes," I nodded, "I saw that. Wasn't it awesome?" I could tell that at this moment nobody thought I could beat that start. And I agreed. I couldn't beat the start. But I knew the race was made up of more than this and I thought I could beat him on the rest of it.

I really wanted to go up to Jeff and tell him how great his underwater work looked. We had been racing each other for years and yet we had never said more than a few words to each other. I like to be friendly with my competitors before a race; it diffuses some of the tension for me. But somehow I was never able to feel that comfortable with Jeff. We only ever met briefly before competitions and didn't really know each other that well. Finally I had something to talk about. I went to find him to tell him how great he looked but unfortunately he left right after his race and I missed him. I wouldn't get my chance.

Embarrassing though it is to admit, there had been times in the past when I secretly hoped the Americans would boycott the Olympics so it would be easier for me to win a medal. But I had to face the fact that the Americans weren't going to go away, so I had to deal with them. I couldn't deny that they were strong and fast. On the contrary, I now welcomed their strength and speed because I could use them as motivation to push me to new heights. I also recognized that while they were looking great, it didn't mean that I wasn't fast and strong too. By delighting in their excellence I was able to delight in my own.

About a week after the dual meet I arrived in the Olympic village in Barcelona. I wanted to spend the last week before my race surrounded by the world's best athletes. As in Seoul, the atmosphere in the village was electric. Every language imaginable was being spoken, virtually every nationality was represented. The village itself was enormous: there were six movie theatres, a private beach, a post office, three banks and even a twelve-lane bowling alley. But the most incredible part about being there was the people. I would sit for hours and watch as athletes from around the world walked by. Some were enormous, some were tiny, but they were all great in their own right, and every one of them had accomplished amazing things just to get here. I had a big, stupid, admiring grin on my face when I walked around the village. This was quite a contrast from my experience in Seoul.

I had two key revelations about excellence in the final stages before my race on July 30th. They both took place at the Olympic pool. The first occurred on one of my training days. In the final days before the swimming starts there is an open block of time when anyone can use the pool. I was getting ready for my workout one day when I noticed the Americans were at the pool as well. While doing my stretches on the pool deck I found myself staring at Jeff Rouse. My old habit of being fascinated with the competition came back and I sat there watching and imitating everything he did. If he stretched his legs I stretched mine to see if I was as flexible. I knew it was obsessive and self-defeating, but I couldn't help myself.

After about ten minutes I decided I had to get over this fixation if I ever wanted a shot at racing him and winning. I headed over to talk to him. I was really nervous about speaking to my

competitor face to face. I had found out earlier
that we were born a day apart so I made a weak
joke about knowing why he was so good,
because he almost shared my birthday. Ha.
Then I really had nothing else to say. There was
an awkward moment when I was going to tell
him how great his start was but then the small
talk began. Are your parents coming to watch?
Do you like the village? Finally Jeff relaxed and
just let loose. Apparently the bus bringing him
to the pool that afternoon had broken down and
he had had to walk the rest of the way. Now his
legs were dead. By the end of our conversation I
found myself consoling him. I was telling him he
would be fine on the day of the race. Talk about
turning the tables.

From that moment on I never looked at Jeff
the same way. The wall between us had crum-
bled. There is a pitfall in paying too much attention, or the wrong kind of attention, to the excellence of others. In admiring Jeff, I had turned
him into some kind of superhuman adversary,
though of course he was just another guy who
got tired and stressed like me. Even heroes are
human. If I was worried about competing
against Jeff in the 100-metre backstroke, then I
was sure he was worried about me, too. Again I
appreciated how good he was, but now, five

days before the race, we finally both seemed to be on a level playing field.

LOPEZ-ZUBERO

The second event took place on the night of July 28th. On this day at the Olympics there was a race, the 200-metre backstroke, that I had a special interest in. By watching the 200 I would have a chance to see most of my competition swim for the first time. Everybody in my event, except Jeff, David Berkoff and me, was swimming in this race.

The favourite was Martin Lopez-Zubero. He lived in Florida, but his father was Spanish and Martin had become Barcelona's home-town hero in the months prior to the Olympics. He held the world record in the 200 and was expected by most to win Spain's first gold medal at these games.

The race was the very last on the program that evening. It was so hot sitting in the stands I had to constantly get up to find some water and escape the sun for a little while. As I was roaming around I saw Martin sitting and stretching in the shade. There was about an hour left before his race started. I watched him for a minute before he looked up at me. Even though we race against each other we are very good friends, and I could see the stress in his eyes. He knew an entire country was waiting for his race. I felt so nervous for him I didn't really know what to say. I wished him luck and smiled, then said it would all be over soon.

I went back to the stands and waited for the race. As the race drew closer the crowd became more and more anxious. With about half an hour to go before the swim there was an enormous roar. I looked at my team-mates and we all shrugged, not understanding the significance of what was going on. The announcer finally came over the system and said in English, "Ladies and gentlemen, please welcome the King and Queen of Spain." Things suddenly made sense. The Royal Family had come to watch the final of the 200-metre backstroke. I looked at my team-mates again. We all had the same look in our eyes. It said: Poor Martin.

Fifteen minutes later the place really started to go crazy. It all began with one woman on the other side of the pool from us yelling out a cheer. In the stands across the way we heard one voice yell "Lopez-Zubero," then she went clap, clap-clap, clap, clap with her hands. It didn't sound like much but the next time she did it there were ten thousand people chanting

"Lopez-Zubero" and stomping their feet or clapping. It was so loud the stands were vibrating. All the athletes and coaches from the different countries were looking at each other with wonder. And once again I thought to myself, "Poor Martin: such a wild outpouring of emotion could be intoxicating, but it might also spook him."

The finalists for the 200-metre backstroke were finally marched out. By now the crowd was so loud you couldn't hear the introductions of the athletes. The race is started in the water, so eventually all the swimmers jumped in and placed themselves in position. I couldn't hear the starting gun because of the noise.

For the first half of the four-length race Martin didn't look great. He looked as if he had the weight of the world on his shoulders. A Soviet swimmer, Vladimir Selkov, and an Italian, Steffano Battistelli, were ahead of him. The crowd was still cheering but they weren't quite as loud. On the third length Martin started to move. He passed Battistelli and took over second position with only one length left to go.

The entire building erupted as the swimmers moved down the last stretch. Martin had less than one length to overtake the Russian if he was to win the race. I was standing by now, along with everybody else, and cheering for

Martin. The royal box was right by where the athletes sat and I remember looking over and seeing the Queen of Spain with her fists in the air yelling at the top of her lungs. Everyone was going crazy.

With thirty metres left Martin caught up to Selkov, the leader. With twenty-five metres left he passed him. He remained there for the rest of the race and hit the wall in first place, winning Spain's first gold medal of the Barcelona Olympics. The crowd was beside themselves, and all the people in the royal box were congratulating each other. It was complete pandemonium, an absolute celebration.

I may have been standing and jumping when Martin hit the wall, but right after the race I felt so odd I had to sit down. I was looking at my feet, my head was in my hands and I had my eyes closed. My team-mates were coming up to me and patting me on the back, trying to comfort me. They were saying, "It's okay. It's okay. He doesn't look that good." But this wasn't what was making me feel so strange.

It is hard to say exactly what hit me. Earlier I had decided that when I watched the races I wouldn't feel scared. I would really try to enjoy others' moments of glory and wait for my chance. On this night, though, I finally felt what it would be like to win. Maybe it was because this was a race I could relate to, or because Martin was a friend of mine, I'm not sure exactly. But something happened. As I sat and watched the medal ceremony I couldn't help myself. I started to cry. Instead of seeing Martin up on the podium, I saw myself.

SUMMARY

Delighting in Others' Excellence

Excellence comes in all forms.

Someone else's excellence does not come at the expense of your own.

By recognizing others' excellence you realize your own potential.

Your competition ultimately comes from within.

"The greatest good we can do for others is not to share OUR riches but to marvel in THEIRS."
ANONYMOUS

Deryk Snelling and the team in Florida
training for the Barcelona Olympics, 1992

I can't believe I did it! Barcelona, 1992

100 M ESQUENA MASCULINS
CERIMÒNIA DELS VENCEDORS
1   TEWKSBURY,MARK   CAN
2   ROUSE,JEFF   USA
3   BERKOFF,D.   USA

DAKTRONICS INC.

The scoreboard with my name at the top!
Barcelona, 1992

Silken Laumann and me at the closing
ceremonies of the Barcelona Olympics

A victory celebration on
Parliament Hill, Ottawa

Receiving the Lou Marsh Trophy for
Athlete of the Year on February 4, 1993,
the day I officially retired from swimming

9

The Difference Between Nearly Right and Exactly Right

"The difference between ordinary and
extraordinary is that little extra."
ANONYMOUS

ON JULY 29TH I WORKED OUT FOR THE LAST time before my Olympic swim. I went in the morning so that I could spend the rest of my time relaxing and getting ready for the following day. I trained in the indoor pool, staying out of the sun. I didn't watch the morning's preliminaries but before I left I looked at the results from the heat swims. Once again I saw that every race was extremely close.

If one single thing stood out at these games it was the narrowing of the gap between the best and the rest of the world. At prior world competitions there had usually been a significant margin between the top two or three swimmers and the other competitors. This wasn't the case at these Olympics. The bottom half among the ranks of players was catching up to the top half. The younger competitors weren't afraid of beating a world record holder or an Olympic champion. They weren't intimidated by someone's past accomplishments; they just went out and swam. The result was that in the evening's final, where eight swimmers qualify, sometimes all eight swimmers were within a stroke of each other right until the last stages of the race. It was impossible to tell who had won unless you looked at the scoreboard for the results.

Simply put, the world had become much more competitive. Super powers like the former East Germany or the United States were no longer dominating the events. Training facilities and quality coaching have become more accessible, so smaller countries are now on a more equal footing with the larger ones. The medals, which used to be shared mainly by eight countries, were now finding their way to more than twenty-five nations.

This made a big impact on me. On the first day of swimming I was shocked by the results. Because it was so close and there were so many surprises, it became clear that anything could happen. As an outsider it reinforced my own ambitions. I still thought I had a shot at winning. On the second day of the swimming, though, there was another very close race at the pool and I thought to myself, "Hmm, silver would be good." I wasn't giving up but it was so close there were absolutely no guarantees. Even some of the legends in swimming, like Matt Biondi, the American world record holder in the 100-metre freestyle and the nineties' version of Mark Spitz, were leaving the pool without going to the medal podium. It seemed as though it would be a feat simply to win any medal. There was not a big difference, in most cases, between the joy shown by the winner and the bronze medallist. Everyone appreciated how significant winning a medal was.

As I went back to the village to spend my last day resting I thought a lot about the way these Olympics seemed to be unfolding. The people who were winning the medals were just going out and swimming. They weren't trying anything special, they just went out and raced. The difference between them and the fourth- to eighth-place swimmers was that their preparation was solid enough that they could stay with the race right to the very last stroke. They were confident enough to believe in themselves when it really counted the most. There are times in competition when you can start strongly and leave the competitors behind, so if you fade there is nobody close enough to catch you. In Barcelona it was impossible to shake the competition. You couldn't just start strongly, you had to finish with the same conviction. It was that close.

With less than twenty-four hours to go, I had to ask myself if I would have the strength and courage the next day to be there with the best in the world. Had I done enough to be competitive in the final few metres of the race?

OH, I ALMOST FORGOT

I sat in my room in the village and really thought about what I had done, especially this year, to get ready for this moment. The scary thing for me was that before I began reflecting I knew there was no more time left. This was it. If I had ignored anything it would come back to haunt me at this moment.

I thought of all the work I had done in the pool. The long hours of training that had been completed successfully. I felt I was in the best shape of my life. I knew I had taken care of the parts of training that were my weak spots—the underwater kick and the strength work. I might still not be the best in the world in these areas but they had improved 100 per cent.

In the final weeks of training in France I had worked tens of hours on my start and my turn. They were as good as they were ever going to be. I had also worked on touching the wall. I knew the last stroke would be very important; this was where I had lost the World Championship. I swam to the wall over and over, making sure I touched the wall high so that if the race did come down to the last stroke my fingernail would touch before my competitors. I didn't think I could have done anything more in the pool.

The only problem was, I knew that all of my competitors from around the world had done similar training in the water. When I was putting in six-hour days training outdoors in Australia they were all probably doing the same thing in another part of the world. This water work was extremely important, but was it enough to make the difference between winning a medal or not?

As I was looking out over the village from my room I thought of all the little things I had done in planning for this race that most people would probably consider irrelevant. These went beyond what I had done in the pool. They were the things I had done to prepare myself for life in the village, and to make myself feel comfortable in the final stages when the real pressure started to build. Coming to see Barcelona in March, training in Australia at Christmas, the way I worked on Dr. Hogg's book. These were the things that perhaps only I had done that would make a big difference tomorrow.

I recognized that in this preparation I had left nothing undone—or at least almost nothing. I had thought out even the smallest details, hoping to be as ready as possible. Because I had been to an Olympics before, I knew what to expect. I didn't have any preconceived ideas of living in a glamorous village. I knew being in an Olympic village during the summer months in Spain could be very unpleasant. I would be surrounded by thousands of athletes, and I would probably be sharing living space with ten other guys. The chances of the room having air conditioning were pretty slim. I didn't want to risk it, so I decided to bring my own fan. This way, no matter what was available when I arrived, I would at least be able to stay cool.

For ten weeks I had lugged this thing around for use in the village. It was a big pain but I figured it was worth it. When everybody else was complaining about the heat I would be laughing.

When we finally arrived in Barcelona everything I had anticipated turned out to be true. We were sharing space with ten other guys and there was no air conditioning. The average temperature was in the high thirties. I had been right to bring a fan.

It was the first thing I unpacked. I pulled it out and plugged it into an adaptor that fit the Spanish electrical outlet and watched with smug satisfaction as the fan began to whir. I was thoroughly impressed with my own foresight.

Less than two minutes later I had a small fire in my room. I had remembered to bring the adaptor but overlooked the converter that changes the voltage from 110 to 220. My fan literally exploded before my eyes while I was still unpacking.

It turned out you could buy fans in the village after all. After ten weeks of telling my teammates how prepared I was, I swallowed my pride and bought one. At least I had been thinking ahead.

PILLOW TALK

I have never been a good sleeper. Even in the quietest room with no light at all, I still toss and turn. This was a great concern to me for the final week I had to stay in the village. How would I ever be able to sleep with all the noise and heat?

There are a few objects that can relieve my insomnia to some extent. One of them is a good pillow.

When I was a kid I had a down pillow that my parents had had forever. It was so worn it moulded to your head when you went to sleep at night, but it finally disintegrated to the point where it had to be thrown out. For years I searched for a similar pillow but couldn't find one anywhere.

In May 1992, I had a swim meet in Vancouver. I was billeted with the Evanetz family, which was a welcome change from staying in hotels. When I went to bed the first night I put my head down on what turned out to be a perfect down pillow that moulded to my head. I had the best sleep I'd had in years.

All I could talk about during my stay was this pillow. I am sure the Evanetzes thought I was crazy, but it was a big deal to me.

At the end of the meet Mrs. Evanetz approached me at the pool and said she had a surprise for me. It was the pillow, and she told me to take it with me to the Olympics. For the rest of the summer I used this old, worn pillow and slept better than I could remember. For the first time ever I actually really slept in the Olympic village, and I was sure that when I went to bed the night before my big race I would sleep—another first. This apparently silly little detail made a huge difference to my sense of preparedness.

WALKING

In swimming we do a crazy thing called tapering. What it means is that all year long we work in cycles. There is a big work cycle in which the bulk of the fitness training is done. Then there is the race cycle in which all the work is transferred into stroke-specific training. Finally there is the rest/active cycle called the taper. In the taper phase we do almost nothing. Every couple of days we will do a sprint or a short burst effort but most of the time is spent sleeping and recovering. Essentially we are storing up all of our energy for that big performance. By the time we arrived in the Olympic athletes' village in Barcelona we would be in the taper phase.

One of the most important things to do in this period is to stay off your legs. You try to avoid walking as much as possible. If your legs are tired and stiff there is no chance of swimming fast.

Staying off your legs is a pretty big challenge in an Olympic village. It is impossible not to walk around. To eat you have to walk to the cafeteria, to catch the bus to the pool you have to walk to the bus stop, etc. I decided the only way to avoid stiffness and muscle fatigue was to become used to walking before I got to the village.

Three months before we left Canada I forced myself to stop driving to and from the pool and start walking. My house in Calgary was a thirty-minute walk from the pool, compared to a five-minute drive. It added an hour to my working day, and at first my legs were really sore, but the more I walked the more my legs got used to the exercise. At the end of the first month I was completely adjusted to walking regularly. I kept this routine for the rest of the summer.

The village in Barcelona turned out to be even bigger than the one in Korea which I had thought was enormous. We all had to do a lot of walking, but this didn't stress me out because I knew that my legs were conditioned for it.

T. G. I. T.

The fact that I had paid attention to minor details gave me reassurance as I was reflecting the night before the swim, an added confidence that I was ready to go. The fan, the pillow and preparing for the walking in the village were little things that would seem insignificant, even laughable, to anyone but me.

There was one more detail I attended to during the year that may have been the most important of all. About six months away from Barcelona, when I found out that I would be swimming on Thursday, July 30th, one of my friends came up with a great idea: I should try to look forward to every Thursday. This way when I woke up on Thursday at the Olympics I would just naturally think of it as being my special day.

This was easier said than done. Thursday was very close to the end of my work week, which started on Monday and ended on Saturday afternoon (I took most Sundays off) and I was usually exhausted by the time it came around. When I first tried to make it my day it just didn't work. I was thinking purely in swimming terms. I would go to workout and swim the practice trying to maintain an enthusiastic outlook, but sometimes the mind and the body don't want to co-operate. As much as I would have loved every Thursday's swimming to have been perfect, a lot of times it just wasn't.

Finally, instead of focusing on Thursday as a great swimming day I started to focus on it as a great day in general. The swimming was only one part of the day. Every Thursday, no matter how I felt, I decided I would do something for myself. I would go out for dinner or see a movie. If there was anything that made me feel good I would try to do it on that day.

At first it required a real effort to make myself look forward to Thursdays. It felt so forced and staged. I saw how adaptable I was, though, because after a few weeks I really felt like it was my day. I kept up this treatment of Thursdays until the week before the Olympics. I just hoped when I woke up on July 30th it would be my special day.

BIG DIFFERENCE

That evening I went down to the enormous common room shared by Canada and Australia in the village and watched the day's swimming finals on TV. When they were all over for the evening I realized this was it. The next set of swimming results would involve me. The waiting was almost over. For the first time ever I wasn't scared the night before my swim. I was excited, but there wasn't the usual anxiety.

I went back to my room and prepared my bag for the morning. I double-checked to make sure I had everything I would need and a back-up just in case. I had my racing suit, goggles, towels, track suits, shorts and my Walkman. Everything was set. My team-mates came by and wished me well, and finally Anne, our team manager, came to make sure everything was okay. I read a few of my favourite cards of encouragement from friends and focused on feeling good about myself before going to sleep.

I felt tremendously peaceful that evening. I knew that whatever happened the next day I would be able to live with it, because with the exception of that little converter for the fan, I had done everything possible to be my best. I could not ask for anything more. It now came down to putting it all together when it really counted. And for the first time before an important race, I fell asleep.

SUMMARY

Paying Attention to Details

The little things can make
a big difference.

Don't ignore what may seem insignificant.

What little things separate you
from the competition?

"Watch the little things;
a small leak will sink a great ship."
BENJAMIN FRANKLIN

10

This Is It

"What matters is not the size of
the dog in the fight, but the
size of the fight in the dog."
COACH BEAR BRYANT

I T HAD BEEN HOT AND SUNNY IN BARCELONA for a week, but when I woke up on the morning of July 30th, the sky was overcast. This was the perfect weather for my race, because the sun wouldn't be shining in my eyes.

I wasn't particularly nervous, even now. I knew my day had finally arrived, the waiting was over. I checked my bag one last time and headed down the stairs of my building. I walked alone to the cafeteria, lost in thought. I prayed that today everything would come together. I stripped my race strategy down to its bare essentials: I wanted to be my best. Little did I know how different my life would be in twelve hours.

The first step was to qualify for the final. I went to the pool and got ready for the heats. There are about sixty swimmers in the 100-metre backstroke in the morning, so fifty-two are eliminated before the top eight swim for the medals in the evening. Realistically, in order to have a shot at winning the gold medal you should be positioned in the top four after the heats. I was going into the Olympics ranked fifth. I would have to improve my position.

The two hours between the end of my warm-up at nine and my heat at eleven were sheer torture. I spent most of the time listening to music on my Walkman, stretching, and trying to calm myself. There was a strange duality; part of me was in control, getting ready for just another race, while the other part of me was trying not to freak out because this was the Olympics and I had waited for this moment for a long, long time. As I was stretching by the indoor training pool I could see the men from the event before mine coming in to do their warm-down. If they were finished it meant my event was up next. My race would be marshalled any minute now. It was time to head to the ready-room area.

With so many men competing in the heats, the marshalling area is very crowded, and the protocol in the morning is much more relaxed than it is at the evening race. All that is required is that you check in when you arrive and show up again when they are ready for your swim. I was in the second last heat, number six, so I had some time before I was up. I went into the hallway just outside the ready room and sat on the floor, continuing my stretches. I was impatient to get on with my swim but I felt good. For ten minutes I pictured the race in my mind. I would be swimming against the second-ranked swimmer in the world, David Berkoff of the US. I saw myself winning the heat over and over again until the image was absolutely clear in my mind. When I felt perfectly focused, I went back into the marshalling area.

At quarter to eleven the seven other swimmers in my heat and I were gathered in the final waiting area, watching the heat before our swim. As the results were announced, I knew that in seconds the Olympic music would start and we would be marched out. I took a few deep breaths and for the last time thought, "This is it!" Before I knew it I was walking in front of the crowd to lane five for my first race at these Olympics.

The heats are very important but there isn't much fanfare surrounding them. The introduction of the swimmers is brief. I barely had enough time to take off my track suit before the referee blew his whistle to indicate it was time to get into the water and take our starting positions. Suddenly I was feeling quite nervous but I was also still very focused.

Competing for the first time at a meet is always a bit unnerving. It usually takes me one race to get all the bugs out. In my heat swim I felt good but I was a bit lost. I was having a hard time gauging where Berkoff, who was beside me in lane four, was throughout the race. In the last fifteen metres I knew we were close. My legs felt really tired and it seemed as though

I was swimming in slow motion. I remember seeing the backstroke flags overhead which meant I had five metres left. I was still unsure where Berkoff was as I took my last two strokes and lunged for the wall. I looked up at the score-board. Beside my name was my time, 54.7, and the number one. I had won the heat and set a new Canadian record. I felt great but also completely exhausted. I didn't know if I had anything left for the final that evening.

I dragged myself out of the pool and went to the side of the deck. I wanted to watch the last heat of our event. In it was Rouse, the world record holder. Jeff swam well but he didn't go nearly as fast as I had thought he would. After his swim the qualifying list for the finals came up immediately. It looked like this:

1. ROUSE, JEFF   USA   54.6

2. TEWKSBURY, MARK   CAN   54.7

3. BERKOFF, DAVID   USA   54.8

In fourth place was the only other real contender, Martin Lopez-Zubero, who was a few tenths behind. The top four backstrokers in the world were within less than half a second of each other.

My mind started spinning. My first thought was of how close my heat time was to Jeff's. My next thought was of how hard physically that heat swim was for me. Would I have enough left in me for this evening? I assumed that my competitors had worked as hard as I had this morning, so nobody could afford to hold back. We were on a level playing field, and it would be a very close final tonight.

If there was ever a chance, this was it. I knew that I would never get an opportunity like this again. I was closer to being the best in the world than I had ever been before. The winner tonight would be decided by hundredths of a second and I was one of the contenders. There was a lot to do in the next eight hours to get ready for this race.

I went immediately to the warm-down pool. It's important after every race to warm down because the lactic acid which builds up in the body after an intense effort will make your muscles tight and sore. Swimming at a medium pace for fifteen to twenty minutes following a race enables you to start flushing this acid out of the system.

When I got out of the pool my coach and team manager were waiting for me, beaming. Deryk gave me a quick analysis of the race and Anne pulled me off to quickly do some interviews. Everybody was so excited because it looked as though we would finally win a medal in the pool.

During the interviews, when Rob Faulds from

CTV asked me what I thought of my chances in the final, I told him I thought I would be either first or fourth. It was a thought I hung onto all day long. I didn't even consider second or third; it was all or nothing. In my excitement I would have done interviews for as long as the reporters wanted, forgetting how tiring they were. But after a couple of minutes I looked up and there was Laurie Lawrence, my coach in Australia, with a concerned look on his face. He was holding up a piece of paper with one word on it: REST. I got the message and finished the interview.

I found that everyone had gone back to the village, except for Anne, who knew I should not be left alone. On our bus ride back to the athletes' village my mind was still churning. I was outwardly very calm but waves of anxiety washed over me because I kept picturing myself winning, and that made me feel sick to my stomach for a second. It was hard to come to terms with the possibility of the dream of a lifetime coming true in a few hours' time. I couldn't stop seeing myself winning. It was so clear in my mind.

I went to the cafeteria with Anne as soon as we got back. I tried to eat but it was very difficult: I was too nervous to swallow, so I decided to try to rest first and eat later. On the way back to my room I called home to let Debbie, my underwater coach, know what had happened. It was five in the morning for her but she picked up the phone on the first ring. I don't think she was sleeping. I told her the results and repeated what I had told CTV—I was going to be first or fourth, I was either going to win the thing or miss a medal entirely. As I was saying this to Debbie I tried to picture myself coming fourth, but I just couldn't see it. From that moment on I thought only about winning. Somebody had to win this race. Why not me?

My room-mates were waiting for me when I got back. They all thought I had a real shot at winning, and gave me of words of encouragement. They then left so I could be alone and have some quiet time. I was finally by myself.

Sleeping was out of the question—I was far too excited—so I just lay on my bed listening to music, and trying to relax. Whenever I tried to think about the race my eyes would tear up. Finally I let myself cry and got rid of all the stress pent up from waiting for so long. When I got up from my rest I felt completely calm; I wasn't scared or emotional any more. Somewhere inside I had come to terms with winning and felt completely focused.

I went back to the cafeteria and had some very bland food that would be easy on my stomach. I still found it difficult to eat but I knew I would need some food energy for my race. It was an important part of my final preparation. All this time I was really in my own little world, oblivious to the thousands of people in the building with me. I just sat down with my food, ate and left.

I headed straight for the buses taking the swimmers back to the pool for the finals. Although there are many things you can plan for, some you can't. As I was getting on the bus I realized that the entire American team was there, occupying at least forty of the fifty-four seats. I wanted to get off and wait for the next bus to avoid a nightmare ride, but decided it would be like waving a white flag to my competitors. I gritted my teeth, held my head high, and walked down the centre aisle to find myself a seat. There were a few seats without bodies in them but the American swimmers had put their bags on these spots. I eventually had to ask a guy to move his bag so I could sit down. He looked at me with contempt but gave way so I could be seated.

As the bus started to pull away, there was a loud bang on the front door. We stopped, the door opened, and on hopped Anne, my guardian for the day. I couldn't help but smile. She made quite an entrance and followed it through by sitting next to me. Every time I needed her she was there.

The pool was situated on Mount Juvic beside the Olympic Stadium, and in the area there were always thousands of people roaming the streets, coming and going to various events. When I got off the bus there was a Canadian group waiting and they let out a big cheer for me as I walked by. I felt so proud to be representing them in the final. I was still very calm and I couldn't wipe an enormous grin off my face.

I went straight to the outdoor competition pool. My final was more than two hours away, so I just sat by the pool stretching during the warm-up period, getting a feel for the atmosphere as people started taking their seats. Then I got into the pool and did a little bit of easy swimming, did a start in lane five, the lane I had qualified in, and called it a day. This was the last swim I would have in this pool before the real thing in two hours' time.

I went to the indoor warm-up pool where I had spent time in the morning and sat with my team-mates who were also swimming that evening. I listened to music again and tried not to think about the race too much. With one hour to go I started my final preparation. I visualized the race over and over in my mind—always winning. Once I was ready mentally I got into the pool for my second warm-up. I didn't swim very much, just loosened up. The fatigue from the morning's race was gone and I felt great. I was ready to go.

Then, forty minutes before the race, it was time to go to the ready room. I went down a little bit early so I could be the first one there—I wanted the other guys to notice me as they came in rather than the other way round. To get to the ready room you had to walk down a long, dark, narrow hallway. It was an intimidating walk because this was really it, I was about to check in for the Olympic final. I took deep breaths as I walked down the corridor. "Relax," I told myself, "relax."

The first thing I did was check in. There was the usual set-up and over the next fifteen minutes all of my competitors arrived. As we were stretching and getting ready, the marshal took us into another area. This was a bit unusual for an international meet. Usually once you are in the ready room you stay there until just before the race. In Barcelona, for the last twenty-five minutes we were held in a small area directly below the stands, beneath thousands of people. There wasn't a lot of room and the atmosphere was intense.

It is at this point that many races are won and lost. You can be the best-trained athlete in the world but if you lose confidence in yourself at this point your chances of winning are all gone. I had been through this process so many times that I knew what to expect. The Americans would lie on the floor, in their track suits, shaking their limbs. Lopez-Zubero would sit in a chair and talk to people, trying to distract them in a friendly way. I would sit in a chair with a towel over my head, visualizing, and then get up and walk around for a few minutes.

While we were in this area we could hear the muffled sounds of the crowd. After a few minutes there was a big cheer. The chief marshal came in and told us the King and Queen of Spain were here. Martin Lopez-Zubero stopped talking.

I watched as the other guys were getting ready and talked to Martin for a few minutes. All the time, I kept taking deep breaths to force myself to relax. I wasn't scared at all, just very excited. I felt better than ever before.

Just before we marched out, the medals were given to the women in the 800-metre freestyle. I remember sitting in my chair as they announced the women's winner, and instead of hearing Olympic champion and gold medallist, representing the United States of America, Janet Evans, I said to myself, representing Canada, Mark Tewksbury. I let it sink in, and my stomach didn't flip.

After the victory walk for the women was completed the chief marshal came in and said, "Gentlemen, please line up for the Olympic final of the men's 100-metre backstroke." He called out our names and we lined up accordingly. I was positioned between Jeff Rouse in lane four and Lopez-Zubero in lane six. This was the best place I could be. It was very quiet as we stood there waiting for our cue. In the distance the music started. This was it. I thought of all the people at home watching and I felt my arms start to tingle with a surge of adrenaline. Before I knew it, we were marched out from this tiny room to the outdoor pool with ten thousand people cheering.

Unlike the informality of the morning there was a lot of protocol before the start of the race. Each competitor is introduced in four different languages so it takes a while. As I was waiting my turn I walked to the end of my lane, number five, and looked down the length of the pool. The first thing I saw was the scoreboard and I found my name. I remembered being here, standing in this exact spot in March, and feeling some comfort from that. I didn't really notice the people in the stands. I thought of the thousands of times I had swum the 100-metre backstroke and reminded myself this was just another race. I heard my name being announced and waved to the crowd. I stood up and did my last stretches and took deep breaths. At last, the announcer finished, the crowd let out an enormous roar and the referee blew his whistle. It was time to get into the water for the start of the race.

This was one of my favourite moments. When I jumped into the water I felt at home. It was cold, twelve feet down, but it was silent, an escape from the noise of the crowd. I stood on the bottom of the pool and shook out, thinking to myself, "Fast and easy," and then I pushed off the bottom. As I broke the surface of the water I heard the Canadians in the crowd cheering wildly and I knew it was for me. I felt completely empowered. I swam up to the starting end and got ready to place my feet against the wall of the pool. As we all got into our starting positions a hush fell over the crowd. I waited for the starter to give us our commands.

Finally, the words came. "Swimmers," he said, "take your marks." I heard the starting gun go off and reacted before I even knew it. I drove off the wall with my feet and flung my arms back to start the race, swimming the first twelve metres underwater. When I surfaced I had no idea for a second where I was in relation to the other swimmers. All I could hear was the roar of the crowd. As things came into focus I realized two things. First, I couldn't see Rouse on my left-hand side. This meant he was ahead of me. That was okay because I knew the start and turn were his strengths. My chance would come in the last part of the race. Second, I saw that I was ahead of Lopez-Zubero on my other side.

As I was moving down the first length I thought simple things like breathe and save your legs for the final stretch. Before I knew it, I saw the backstroke flags and I was halfway through the race. I did a flip turn and swam seven or eight metres underwater. As I came up out of the turn I said two words to myself: Go NOW! As I started to really swim, I felt a splash at the side of my head. It was Jeff's foot—not a good sign. But I remained entirely focused, saying "Go now!" with each stroke I took. As the race progressed I could feel the splash from Jeff's kick move from my head, to my chest, to my waist, until finally it was down at my knees. I was catching the world record holder.

At the 85-metre mark I usually die. I am physically exhausted at this point in the race, but in Barcelona I said to myself, "Go Again!" I saw Jeff's hand out of the corner of my eye and I knew I was only a tiny bit behind him. With ten metres to go I could see I was catching up to him. I was still totally focused, and now I knew once and for all that I could win this race. I had been in races this close before and lost. It could go either way. With five metres left to go I couldn't see him any more because we were dead even. I had two strokes left. I pulled with my right arm and as fast as I could, reached with my left arm and touched the wall with my fingertips.

The first thing I did, as always, was to look up at the scoreboard. I grabbed the end of the pool and held myself up out of the water. Because the race was so close the electronic signal from the touch pad to the scoreboard momentarily jammed. I remember waiting for the results to come up and literally holding my breath. I didn't see the number one, I didn't see my time, but, finally, I saw my last name blink. It blinked first, which meant I had won the race.

Like anybody who has just had their dream come true, I totally lost control. Somehow I ended up sitting on the lane rope five metres away from the wall. It was here that it really hit me. I had not just won a race, I had won Olympic gold. I grabbed my head in shock. The other swimmers in the race came over and congratulated me. Martin Lopez-Zubero looked me in the eyes and said, "You did it. Feels pretty good, huh?" I didn't know. I couldn't feel yet.

We exited the pool and I looked up at the scoreboard. Before today, my personal best for the 100-metre backstroke had been 55.19. On the scoreboard, beside my name, the time was 53.98. I had dropped over a second on the day. This morning if somebody had asked me what it would take to win I would have guessed 54-something. I never even considered making such a big drop. I just thought I could win the race on this day. My focus wasn't on numbers but on the other competitors. Beside Jeff's name was the time 54.04. I had won the race by six one-hundredths of a second. Who's to say that paying attention to details doesn't matter?

I went from the pool to a tiny room, similar to the ready room, where the winners wait for the medal ceremony. Everybody there was in shock. I was in shock because I had won, Jeff was in shock because I had won, and David Berkoff was in shock because he had won a medal, the bronze. We all walked around looking like lost kids, bumping into each other. I looked at the entrance to the room and there was Anne, who had been there every step of the way today, holding the track suit I was to put on for the ceremony. She was crying as she said, "I knew you were going to do it, honey." I squeezed her hand and said, "I know you did."

My throat was so dry I could barely speak. I was numb. Three Spanish women came into the room with the medals, and we lined up behind them. Again, as before the race, we were very quiet. In the distance I could hear the victory ceremony music start as we began to walk. I couldn't stop smiling.

Even when they placed the medal around my neck it still didn't seem real to me. I looked up at my team-mates in the stands and shrugged my shoulders. This couldn't really be happening. I looked right at Marcel Gery and we both laughed; this was unbelievable. The emotions didn't hit me until they asked the crowd to stand for the playing of Canada's national anthem. As I watched the flag being raised and started to sing "O Canada," I realized they were playing it for me. I made it through the first two lines and that was it.

One of my favourite memories of the day is of the victory walk around the pool. As I passed the stands where my team-mates were sitting, they all went crazy. What made it even better was that athletes from other countries were cheering, too. They had seen me around the international scene for eight years but never seen me win. Finally, when it counted the most to me, it had happened. The German team did a cheer, "Bravo, Mark." The Australians and Europeans gave me the thumbs up. This meant so much coming from my peers. On the very last stretch of the walk we passed the ready room and saw the competitors for the next race, the women's relay. As I went by, a lot of the women had tears of joy in their eyes.

From this moment on it was absolute pandemonium. I was led to a press conference with Jeff and David in a room the size of a classroom. There were many familiar faces in the front row—Marty Knack from the *Edmonton Journal*, Christie Blatchford from *The Toronto Sun*, and Rosie DiManno from *The Toronto Star*. I was so excited about winning that I felt like exploding but I tried to remain composed. I wanted to make sure that I didn't ramble on and make the other two medallists feel awful. I had been in their shoes so many times throughout my career that I could appreciate what they were going through. We were interviewed for more than half an hour but it went by very quickly.

Then I went with Anne to the drug-testing centre to give a urine test to make sure I was drug free. I still felt very excited but Jeff was being tested as well and he looked pretty devastated, so I tried to stay low-key. Lopez-Zubero, who was also being tested, kept looking at me and smiling. He knew how I was feeling.

The rest of the night was a blur, warming down, seeing Deryk and my team-mates, arriving at the village.

Finally I went back to my room. I was very drained but knew that even though I had to swim tomorrow there was no chance I would sleep tonight. I was in another world. For the first time since the race, I was alone with my medal. I pulled it out of its case and really looked at it. It was truly magnificent—big, heavy, solid—and it was mine.

11

And the Beat Goes On...

THE FOLLOWING MORNING, JULY 31ST, I SWAM in the medley relay, and that evening our team won a bronze medal in the last race of the Olympic swimming competition. When the day was over I could finally let down emotionally. It was hard for me to absorb all that had happened over the previous two days. In my wildest dreams I had imagined winning, and my vision had taken me as far as the medal podium. But I had never really thought about what would happen next.

At the Olympics we swimmers are fortunate because we are among the first to finish competing. All of our events are completed after the first week, which leaves us more than ten days to watch the other events. It's a chance to marvel at the atmosphere of the Olympics without having to deal with the pressure. For ten glorious days I watched the rest of the games, spending most of my time shuttling between the Olympic stadium and the Olympic pool, watching the track-and-field events and synchronized swimming. I was in the stands when Mark McCoy won his gold medal in the 110-metre hurdles. I also watched as Sylvie Frechette won her silver medal in synchronized swimming. Every time I went to an event and heard the victory ceremony music, it made me feel fantastic all over again.

In the evenings I would go out and celebrate. If there was ever a city that could host the world's biggest party, it was Barcelona. When the competitions were over, there was an amazing camaraderie among all the athletes. We had gone through similar experiences leading up to the games, and when the discipline of training and the stress of competing were finally lifted we formed a great bond with each other. Whether you had come in first or fiftieth became irrelevant. The important thing was that you were there. In the village you are surrounded by athletes who have won medals. You become one of many, lost in the crowds. Maybe this is why coming home was such a shock.

On August 10th I travelled from the closing ceremonies to the airport in Barcelona for the flight home. Most of the team was travelling through Toronto later in the day, but there was a small group of us who were heading to the west coast and landing in Vancouver. To meet this flight, we had to make a connection in London, England. I will never forget boarding the plane at Gatwick Airport. One of the stewardesses said, "There he is, the guy from *Time*." I had no idea what she was talking about until Anne, who was still with me, opened a magazine. When I heard her scream, I looked, and there I was on the cover of *Time* magazine. I couldn't believe it. My first reaction was to grab the magazine and shove it into the pocket in front of me. It was so weird to see the face I saw in the mirror every morning on the cover of *Time.*

Until then I hadn't really thought about what it would be like when I got home. I had seen so many things at the Olympics, been to so many events, that my win seemed to have happened ages ago. I never considered what everyone at home was thinking when I won. Seeing that magazine cover gave me a little taste of what was going to happen to my life over the next few months.

From the day I arrived in Calgary, everything was different. Instead of training at the pool, as I had done almost since I could remember, I spent my first morning at a "wardrobe call" for a commercial. Me in a commercial. Who would have thought? There were endless interviews, and suddenly I realized I was booked solid every day, speaking, visiting schools, appearing in shopping centres for the next month. I don't remember a lot about this period because I went on autopilot. I had worked so hard building up to the games with the thought that in August the work and commitment would all be over.

Now I found it was just starting and there was no end in sight.

In the fall I attended a lot of banquets, sales meetings and seminars where I was asked to be the guest speaker. At some of the functions other medallists from the Olympics were present. Again and again the athletes asked me, "Have you gone through the down-time yet?" I answered "No," but thought to myself, "What down-time? I'm living the perfect life." I knew from coming home in 1988, after Seoul, that it was very common to go through a difficult time after the electric high of the Olympics. What I didn't know was that it wasn't necessarily coming down from the games that brings on this depression, but rather, if you're not going back to your sport, the realization that something you have worked for most of your life is over once and for all. Many athletes experience an empty feeling when they realize this, but for a long time I didn't. Unlike others, I immediately had a new focus. I was speaking to thousands of people weekly, touring the country and working with sponsors. There wasn't time to be depressed or reflective. I went through some readjusting, but it was based more on getting used to being recognized than on finding a new direction for my life.

I wish now that I had had a television crew following me during this period because it was truly unbelievable. One day I would be speaking to fifteen hundred people in Vancouver and the next day I would be signing hundreds of autographs in a department store in Toronto. Everywhere I went there were crowds of people lined up to see me. This took a lot of getting used to. I was only a swimmer, for crying out loud, not a Hollywood star. Six months earlier when I had done some store appearances for one of my sponsors, I had had to beg people to come up and talk to me and get autographs. Now I had to be escorted by two security guards to get to the table where I was supposed to do my signing. I found it very hard to absorb the fact that this was my life and would be so for the foreseeable future.

During this period I took things one day at a time. If I was going to keep my sanity, there really was no other option. I appreciated that things had changed, but I didn't want to change through living in this circus. I was still the same kid I had been six months earlier.

Gradually, though, I began to adapt to my situation. I don't know if anyone ever gets used to living like this but I decided this was a chance of a lifetime and I would go with it for a while. The hardest thing to get used to was the lack of privacy. As an amateur athlete I was relatively unknown. I could do day-to-day things without anyone taking notice. That wasn't the case any more. Everywhere I went, people referred to me by name. It was great that I had touched so many people, but in many ways I was a private person and I found it hard to give up my anonymity.

I had thought from the beginning that this crazy time would last, at most, until December. Over Christmas I realized things weren't changing. The new year wasn't a lot different from the last half of 1992. By mid-February I was booked with speaking engagements and appearances for the rest of 1993. Somewhere along the way I had lost control. I felt as though I was riding on a train that was running on its own steam and I didn't know how to get off. My life was becoming a circus.

It was incredible to me that there was no middle ground in this field. Either you are in demand, which means you are busy all the time, or you are not, which means you would kill for sponsors and some support. I had been in both positions and found them both less than perfect.

The really hard thing about this period was that I couldn't find anybody to talk to or share my thoughts with. Who would believe that living this apparently glamorous lifestyle wasn't a dream come true? I was ashamed that at times I was unhappy when most athletes would do anything to be in my position. I felt very alone. Even though I had people around me, it was impossible to explain exactly what it was like, even to them. There are, of course, some great moments in touring, but there is also an incredible responsibility that comes with the job. This was sometimes hard to deal with. I found it difficult to live up to people's expectations of me. When I was with friends I would become frustrated because the conversation always revolved around me. Everybody found the attention I was receiving wonderful, but they didn't understand that it was hard to live like this day after day.

I almost lost it a couple of times. I started to feel as though I didn't really belong anywhere. My frustrations would surface, but I wouldn't let them come to a head. In January I started to have bad days when I felt depressed. I would fight it, though, and go through these times on autopilot, as I had in the fall. In February the number of bad days increased but I kept running from my feelings. When I looked despairingly at my schedule I refused to think of breaking any of my commitments. A lot of people were depending on me to be at various events across the country.

By the end of February when I attended a banquet in Montreal, I was getting very close to the edge. At the time I was so exhausted from my travel schedule and deadlines for this book that I could barely think. Luckily, Silken Laumann, the rower who had fought against incredible odds to win a medal, was at the banquet as well. I really needed to open up to someone and if there was anyone I could talk to, it was Silken. She too had been going through a similar period, so I could finally talk to someone without feeling embarrassed or ashamed. She could empathize with everything I was saying because she felt the same way. Our lives had changed so quickly that things didn't seem real. We sat and shared stories and for the first time in months I laughed, really laughed from my gut, and felt like my old self. After seeing Silken I felt recharged for a while, but I was still running from the real problem.

In March, the wall finally came. It hit me in a way I could never have imagined. I became so stressed that when I went to give a speech in front of thousands of people I couldn't think. My mind went blank. In all my years of speaking this had never happened before. It was such an awful feeling, looking out into the crowd and having absolutely no idea what I was going to say next. The silence was unbearable as I realized they were waiting for me to say something, anything, and all I could think was, "I'm dying up here." It was time for a break.

I cancelled all of my commitments for two weeks to give myself some time to sort things out. I reflected a lot during this break. When I came home from the Olympics in 1988 I had been disappointed with my performance. There was a really tough period in the following months when I had to figure out what I wanted to do with my life. I always thought that that down-time had come because I had placed fifth in the Olympic final. I now realized that this period would have come anyway, even if I had won. After completing an enormous cycle working towards a goal, my mind and body needed time to recover. After making it to the very top of the world, there had to be some low times to keep things in balance. It was inevitable.

After Barcelona, I hadn't given myself the time needed to go through the natural low period. For four years I had put extreme amounts of effort into working towards one specific thing, and when it was finally over there should have been a re-adjustment period. I never gave myself the chance to come down. I reached my ultimate dream, but I wanted that high to last forever. I didn't ever come back to reality before I started this new life.

Finally I stopped beating myself up for being depressed and realized I was human. There wasn't anything wrong with me; I just didn't have any sense of balance. In less than three months, everything in my life had changed. I went from being unknown to being a celebrity, a commodity and a role model; from swimming six hours a day to never swimming at all. Instead of being with a team most of the time, I was alone. I travelled by myself, I worked out by myself. I spent 90 per cent of my time away from home. I felt completely out of control and depressed because I was lost. I didn't have a sense of who I was any more.

Part of the problem was the actual swim in Barcelona. The way I picture the race and the way it was seen on TV are two completely different images. When I watch my Olympic race on video it seems as if that is a different person up there. I see a guy who was lucky enough to have had the most remarkable day, a perfect day. Unfortunately, it is impossible to have that kind of moment or to be that kind of guy every single day. This haunted my thoughts. I didn't want to think that at age twenty-five the best thing that was going to take place in my life had already happened. What a terrible thought! With things now in a better perspective I realize there is a lot more waiting for me out there. Before I can go after it, though, I will need to return to the basics.

In my everyday life I must regain the balance that took me to the top in swimming. I now see the Olympics in a very different light. I have this wonderful memento, a gold medal, to remind me for the rest of my life about my experience. The medal is important, but not as an end in itself. The medal is important because it is a product of the process that took me to the top. This is what was so special about the Olympics to me. I learned the skills and tools necessary to overcome great odds and be the best I could be. This is worth far more than gold.

Before I can feel satisfied again I know I must go back to what I did as an eight-year-old child. I must find something that really interests me and start dreaming about it. I must have a new focus so that I have a sense of vision and direction again. It may take a while to find something, but I know when it is time it will happen. In the interim I will set short-term goals to get me through this upcoming period. Very few of us ever get a chance to make a real difference in the lives of a lot of people. Right now, with my motivational speeches to schools and businesses, I hope I am making a difference. I will continue to take that gold medal and share my story for the next while.

With this goal in mind, my actions make a lot more sense to me. I understand why I am on the road so much, why I make the speeches, because it is important to do this work right now. I also know that sometimes the dream follows the actions. I was fortunate to find my first dream when I was so young, but maybe this time the vision will follow the action rather than the other way around. I am asked frequently, "What next?" I really don't know, but with time it will come. In the interim I will continue to live by the principles I believe in.

One of the most important things I have learned is to like what you do. I couldn't do something that I really didn't like day after day. I couldn't fake it. This doesn't mean every day is perfect. On the contrary, most days can be difficult. I just know that for as many times as I didn't want to go to the pool, deep inside I appreciated how challenging it was. I loved the prospect that every day could be better than yesterday if I rose to the challenge. Whatever it is that I end up doing, I will do it well. If it is worth doing, no matter what it is, it is worth doing well.

When I officially announced my retirement from swimming on February 4th, 1993, there was much more than just a physical void left. More than anything I miss the people who surrounded me. As much as we disagreed, I really miss my coach, Deryk. He was filled with passion and believed to the very end that what he was doing was the best possible solution to get me to the top. Even though we questioned each other a lot of the time, we were always working towards the same goal. We shared a common mission that was stronger than both our personalities. I miss that relationship. It taught me the importance of being coachable, coupled with the maturity to be ultimately accountable to myself.

I also miss my team-mates. They were such an enormous part of my success. It is rare to find a group of people who share the same vision as you. They made my victories—and my defeats—that much better because I had people to share them with. I have seen that, for me, it is impossible to be successful without a strong support group. As I am finding my new path I know that in addition to my current support group, I will find new friends to keep me motivated and on track when I want to give up.

I look back at swimming, and at sport, with great fondness. I realize that they have affected my life in a big way. Over the years my sport taught me much more than going back and forth in a pool, and helped mould me into the person I am today. It instilled in me values which are the very essence of my being, principles that I believe in and stand up for. Sport has given me character, and shown me examples of courage and discipline that I greatly admire in other people and have tried to echo in my own life. I have seen many champions in my time but the true winners to me were always the ones who bore their victory with humility and grace.

I understand that no matter what road I choose in life there will be hard times. I also know that anything worth having is worth working for. Nothing comes easily but that is what will make it so much better when I do achieve my next dream. I will appreciate how difficult it was and celebrate that much more.

I think there are certain ingredients that are common to all successes. First, it is impossible to avoid the work. This is the money in the bank that accumulates over the years. It is from the work that we draw our knowledge and experience, and this takes time. Things very rarely change overnight, but somehow time has a way of giving a new perspective to a situation. To wait takes patience. I have seen the patient, driven man who has not given up become the Olympic champion.

Most importantly, I know I must remain true to myself. I must find what I want to do with my life and tackle it. Life is too short to tiptoe through it. During the entire Olympic year I had one great advantage over many of my competitors. I knew that was the time of my life. I knew that no matter how arduous my path, life didn't get any better than that. I was being challenged to be my best every single day. What more could I ask for?

I can see now that this is still the time of my life. As with my own career, which started because I watched the 1976 Olympics on TV, I know there are thousands of kids who have started in sport because of the 1992 Olympic team, and I am a part of that. That memory never has to fade, even though I now know life is not just about the great times. The most important thing to realize is that this is it. It doesn't get any better than this because it is all I have got. Life is worth more than waiting for something better to come along tomorrow.

If the principles I've communicated in this book hold any truth, which I'm convinced they do, it is possible to live excellence every day. I believe in my life. Believe in yours too.